HEINRICH HEINE reflected the passion. contradictions of his era. A romantic, his verse did much to undermine Romanticism. He was a German who lived half his life in France, a Jew who became a convert to Christianity in order to obtain advancement from a reactionary government which could not in any event accept his liberalism.

Born in 1797 in Düsseldorf, Heine received Jewish religious instruction from a private school and an introduction to the French enlightenment from a Jesuit lyceum. A wealthy uncle in Hamburg tried to set the young man on the path of business, and when that failed, supported his university education at Göttingen and Berlin. At the former Wilhelm Schlegel first took an interest in Heine's verse, and at the latter Hegel instructed him in philosophy.

Twice Heine fell in love with cousins, but he finally married a Parisian *grisette* in 1841 after having lived with her for six years. In his fifty-ninth year he died in Paris, where he had moved permanently in 1831, from a dreadfully painful spinal disease.

ERNST FEISE, the translator of these poems, was born in Germany and holds degrees from the universities of Berlin, Munich, and Leipzig. He is professor emeritus of German language and literature at The Johns Hopkins University.

Lyrische Gedichte Und Balladen

Heinrich Heine

Übersetzt von Ernst Feise

University of Pittsburgh Press

Lyric Poems and Ballads

Heinrich Heine

Translated by Ernst Feise

McGraw-Hill Book Company, Inc.
New York   Toronto   London

ACKNOWLEDGMENTS

Thanks are due the following periodicals and publishers for permission to reprint the translations indicated by title: Monatshefte (The University of Wisconsin): *Lorelei;* The Germanic Review (Columbia University): *Netherworld V;* Preface (Goucher College) and An Anthology of German Poetry (Doubleday & Co., Anchor A 197); *The Slave Ship;* German Life and Letters (Basil Blackwell, Oxford): *The Asra* and five poems from *Lazarus.*

HEINRICH HEINE
1797-1856

From his marble pedestal in the *Cemetery of Montmartre* a German poet looks down with wistful eyes upon the faded flowers brought to his grave from time to time by friends from his fatherland, which has steadfastly denied him a place upon its own soil.

Mons martyrum—even the name of that graveyard seems a reminder of the tragic and paradoxical undertone of his life. He was a German and lived in France half of his years; he was a Jew and renounced the religion of his fathers. He loved his German tongue and was exiled into an idiom not his own; he had a genuine feeling for the sufferings of the Jews and was their sharpest critic. A Romantic poet, he destroyed Romanticism. An aristocrat in spirit, he fought for the suppressed and deprived. A lover of life, he fell victim to a long and horrible disease; a despiser of commercialism, he accepted money from those who had grown rich through it. He was a republican by inclination, but upheld monarchic principles; a renegade who returned to the faith. A poet of love, he was a slave to its lower passions; a lover of truth, he betrayed it to his wit, which spun legends around his enemies, real and imagined. He was a child of his time and believed he was leading it to a better future. His verses were hated and adored; poets of all statures imitated them throughout the nineteenth century even to our day. In French- and English-speaking countries his place after or beside Goethe in lyric poetry was never seriously disputed, but in his homeland it is still a subject of acrimonious debate, which may never subside.

Heinrich Heine was born of Jewish parents, December 13, 1797, in the Rhenish city of Düsseldorf, at the time of the revolutionary French occupation, which brought civil equality to the Jewish community; he died in Paris, February 17, 1856, followed to his grave by a cortège of French authors, artists, composers, and a semi-illiterate wife. Half of his life he had been in voluntary exile from his homeland, which he loved and whose citizenship he had never renounced while he attacked it in bitter verse and prose for its lack of liberty. He grew up between beloved parents: a fastidious, handsome father of little culture and no business sense; a well educated, rationalistic mother, who admired Rousseau but feared that her son might become a poor devil of a poet, dying in the poorhouse. An old nurse kindled his imagination with German folklore, ancient ballads and songs; a private school took care of his Jewish religious instruction; and a Jesuit lyceum introduced him to the freethinkers of the French enlightenment. In his spare time he devoured the current thrillers of knight and robber tales and his first verses inclined toward the spectral and lurid of romantic poets and graveyard phantasies.

These are paradoxes enough for a young soul, but his quick and facile mind had so far been able to cope with such heterogeneous experiences. They sharpened his wit into a protective weapon for his easily wounded sensitivity. Now, however, a sudden removal of the seventeen-year-old youth into the cold and prosaic commercialism of an unsuccessful apprenticeship—first in Frankfort, then in Hamburg—proved to be a severe shock. When his millionaire Uncle Salomon, the famous Hamburg banker, set him up in a draper's firm of his own, he failed again, neglected his duties, wrote poetry instead, and developed a brazen insolence even toward his benefactor, a self-made man of scant culture who remarked when he detected verses of his nephew in a Hamburg newspaper that if the silly boy had learned anything he wouldn't have to write. Nor did he appreciate it when Heine later on dedicated a book to him, and even had the effrontery to say: "The best thing about you, Uncle, is that you bear my name."

The rôle of a good-for-nothing poor relation in this nouveau riche family was, no doubt, hard to bear for Henry—or Harry as he was called then; moreover, he had the misfortune to fall in love successively with his two cousins: Amalie, who refused his fervent advances, and her younger sister Therese, who may have lacked the courage to give in to her warmer feelings for the poor admirer. Perhaps she never did love him although, if we believe the plaints of his verses, his passion lasted a life time.

In good Jewish tradition Uncle Salomon consented to finance his nephew's academic career and allowed him to take up law at the universities of Bonn, Göttingen, and Berlin (1819-1825). The greater part of his time, however, was devoted to writing and to a diligent study of German history, literature, and philosophy under such men as Sartorius, Bopp, Hegel, and August Wilhelm Schlegel. Schlegel, in fact, took a special interest in

Heine's poetry and taught him the art of a relentless self-criticism in poetic composition and versification. As a member of a Burschenschaft, a patriotic student fraternity, he soon began to realize that he was somewhat misplaced in the camp of Teutonic nationalists and that the sufferings of his own, the Jewish people, throughout the ages might furnish him a more romantic subject than medieval Minnesang with a devotion to dame and Nôtre Dame; but his unfinished novel, *The Rabbi of Bacherach,* and his *Hebraic Melodies* belong to later periods of his work. The theme of a people rising again and again from foreign subjection, however, easily associated itself with Friedrich Hegel's philosophy of history and religion. According to Hegel, Heine's teacher in Berlin, God was the self-realization and unfolding of the world-spirit *(Weltgeist)* in history's peculiar progress from thesis to anti-thesis, and their fusion in synthesis, the triadic development arising from recurrent dialectic contradiction to every preceding phase of civilization. According to Hegel, the three ancient religions: the nationalistic Jewish hierarchy (originally a childlike cult of Jehovah), the anthropomorphic aristocracy of the gods in the Greek cult of beauty, the stern and cunning deified state of the Romans were superseded by the realm of Christ, the proclaimer of an all-embracing love. With Christ the spirit of fraternity, equality, and liberty of all humanity had descended upon earth from God's heavenly throne. (p. 61ff)

Here are the roots of Heine's alternating praise and criticism of Christianity and Judaism on the one hand, Hellenism on the other. He fused the Jewish and Christian religions under the name of Nazarenism into a world of caritas: the feeling and commiseration for the afflicted, indigent, and oppressed. But this Nazarenism seemed to atrophy the life of the senses and devaluate the here in favor of the hereafter, thus evading a vigorous fight for social justice on earth. Hellenism, in contrast, meant for Heine the harmonious, esthetic, and hedonistic life in beauty, which he craved but which he also found wanting in human love and social devotion. These were the problems of immediate import to him, and during all his life he suffered from the irreconcilability of those two fundamental attitudes.

At the end of his studies, before taking the doctor's degree in July 1825, Heine found himself compelled to make a religious decision from a practical point of view. As a Jew he could not expect to obtain an official position such as he aspired to, especially since

Prussia had rescinded again the civil rights of Jews in 1823. Therefore he joined the Protestant church even though he was in conscience opposed to any organized and state religion, and his bitterness against both creeds was increased when Christians and Jews alike denounced his baptism. Moreover, his hopes for a special position were as insubstantial as they were naive. What state would have wished to engage the services of an unpredictable poet, a natural rebel in those days of reaction of the Holy Alliance and its fears of subversive demagogues? For a professorship of literature (such as he envisaged in Berlin or Munich) his study of law was hardly an adequate preparation; for his practice of law in Hamburg his sentimental and satiric poetry was not a favorable recommendation. He had nothing except the meager income from his writings; he was nothing except the author of the *Buch der Lieder, (Book of Songs, 1827)*, which in time was to make him one of the great poets of world literature, but whose first edition, five thousand copies, took more than ten years to be sold out.

Yet he was conscious of his poetic eminence, and rightly so. The collection, containing all the poems he had written since he was nineteen, was to become in time one of the events in the history of lyric poetry. It begins with his early songs, ballads, and sonnets, and contains the two forceful ballads *Die Grenadier* and *Belsazar*. The second section, *Lyric Intermezzo*, already shows the typical Heine song of few stanzas, each consisting of four tetrameter lines, trochaic or iambic, with varying rhyme patterns. They stem from the folksong and its adaptation by Wilhelm Müller, the poet of so many of Franz Schubert's compositions. Characteristic for Heine's *Lied* is its nature symbolism, its parallelisms and antitheses, its witty or ironic endings, all hidden under an apparent casualness and a simple, everyday wording and syntax. It reaches its full flowering in the next section, the *Songs of Homecoming (Heimkehr)*, written in 1823 and 1824. Here it unfolds all the richness of its potentialities, the surprising variation of its simplicity in composition, rhythm, and rhyme as well as the variety of its content: sentimental love plaint, tragic or cynical accusation of the beloved or of the trite and philistine world around him, exultation and despair, miniature land and sea scapes, small family scenes and terse little balladesque sketches, often with abrupt changes from mirth to utter despondency, from desolate lament to ludicrous platitude—Heine's famous rupture of mood *(Stimmungsbruch)*. The final section presents the majestic *Chants of the North Sea,* rhymeless hymns, a new vehicle for the changing moods of man and sea and Hegelian phantasies in mythical incarnation.

New, moreover, was the artful composition of the whole book, the arrangement of its sections into smaller cycles, into verse romances and novelettes, weighed against each other as to crescendos and diminuendos, tragic adagios, adoring andantes and jesting or cynical scherzos, a virtuose structure of intricacies, leitmotifs, and surprises. Their sentimentality, perhaps also their arrogance, has palled on us, but a close analysis reveals their art, and if we attempted to anthologize the book, it would quickly disclose its crafty web and discourage our undertaking, for it is an organic entity.

Heine's lyrics are paralleled by his *Travel Pictures (Reisebilder)* in scintillating prose, a genre developed by the movement known as Young Germany. Here romantic lament for a past world of the fortunate few who lived in palaces and castles alternates with a strident demand for a better though more prosaic world of the exploited many. But lest the reader tire of the succession of these two attitudes, the author seasons his travel reports with descriptions of landscapes and people and with witty or melancholy phantasies and reminiscences. From the happy idyls and mild satire of his tramp through the Harz Mountains *(Die Harzreise, 1826)* Heine proceeds to the aggressive critique of social stratification and its abuse in North Sea resorts *(Die Nordsee III, 1827)*, and finally to a bold attack on nobility, state, church and positive religion, and an ardent plea for the liberation of all subject peoples *(Travel Pictures III, 1830)*.

It really seems [we read in his Italian Journey] as if at present people were fighting more over spiritual interests. Daily the foolish national prejudices disappear more and more; all harsh peculiarities tend to fade out in the universality of a European civilization. There are no longer nations, but only parties, and it is a remarkable fact how well these parties, in spite of their various colors and their differences of language, recognize and understand each other. Just as there are state politics dictated by material interests, there are party politics of a spiritual character. Just as state politics would turn even the smallest armed conflict breaking out between two insignificant powers into a general European war (in which all states would have to take part more or less fervently, but in any case interestedly), no minor struggle could now arise anywhere in the world whose general spiritual implications one faction or the other would not at once recognize and in which the remotest and most heterogeneous parties would not be forced to take sides pro or contra. On account of these party politics, be it state or spiritual politics, two great

camps emerge who face each other with hostile words and gestures. . . .
Even though their minds may err, their hearts, nevertheless feel what
they want; and Time presses with her great task.

What then is this great task of our Time?

It is emancipation. Not merely that of the Irish, Greeks, Frankfort
Jews, West Indian Blacks and such oppressed peoples, but the emancipation of the whole world, especially of Europe, which has come of age
and tears loose from the iron leashes of the privileged, the aristocracy
. . . as long as this aristocracy can not convince us that they were born
with spurs on their heels and the others with saddles on their backs, as
Voltaire has said. Every age has its task and through its solution humanity progresses. The former inequality, created through the feudal system
in Europe, was perhaps necessary or a requisite condition of the progress
of civilization, but in our time that progress is impeded by it and civil-
ized hearts rise up against it. . . . Revolution has become a signal for
humanity's war of liberation.

These were bold words in the period of the Holy Alliance, and
it was also bold thinking when Heine changed Hegel's idea of the
inexorable course of a *Weltgeist* to that of the *Zeitgeist* (spirit of
the time), whose progress seemed to him no less relentless and
whose herald and interpreter he believed himself to be. But the
expression of such ideas could not possibly further any plans
Heine had for a position in Catholic Bavaria, the supposed liberal
leaning of its King notwithstanding. The Italian Journey, con-
tained furthermore an attack on a fellow poet, Count Platen, whom
Heine erroneously suspected of being a spokesman of a Munich
group inimical to his interests. Platen, without real provocation,
had written a satirical play in which he ridiculed Heine as a Semite
and a poetaster. Heine, always ready for a lusty combat in which
he could display his superior wit, accepted the challenge and laid
out his aggressor with such unsavory retaliation that he was conscious of a Pyrrhic victory. Moreover, he could entertain no doubts
that the almighty Metternich, the guardian angel of the European
reaction, though he was delighted with the *Buch der Lieder,*
might some day find a nice quiet retreat for its author where he
could write more poetry of its kind instead of inflammatory political articles. So, when the July revolution in France broke out and
drew liberty-loving exiles from all over Europe to Paris, Heine
decided to turn his back on the fatherland, which he was never to
see again except on two short visits, in 1843 and 1844.

In May 1831 Heine arrived in Paris. Except for regular summer
vacations at sea resorts on the English channel, such as he had

also frequented in Germany since 1825 on account of his recurrent headaches, or at Spas of the Pyrenees, the metropolis of the free world became his permanent abode, and his first years there were probably the happiest time of his life. He reveled in the splendors of the *ville de lumière* with its unexcelled theaters and operas, its rich museums, its gay boulevards, and the public balls of the demi-monde. The intellectual salons received with open arms the brilliant prosaist of the *Reisebilder,* the witty sentimentalist of the *Lieder,* the sarcastic political poet. Although his mastery of the word was exiled into a language in which he was never to gain a proficiency measuring up to his literary standards, flashes of his *esprit* circulated among the lovers of a *bon mot;* and writers like Gérard de Nerval, Saint-René Taillandier, and Philarète Chasles came to his aid in translating his poetry and prose. Artists, composers, and scholars opened their circles to this German Musset; ladies of social distinction, such as the beautiful Princess of Belgiojoso courted his friendship; Balzac honored him with the dedication of one of his novels; and Théophile Gautier became a lifelong friend. It was, however, not a woman of literary rank and amorous reputation, like George Sand (whose merits he extolled in one of his articles),who was to cast a lasting spell of love upon him, but a low-born, high-spirited Parisian *grisette,* Crescentia Eugénie Mirat, who entered upon a somewhat tempestuous union with him in 1835, which was legalized in 1841. She knew and understood nothing of his poetry, shared none of his intellectual interests but much of his hard earned money (and the gifts of Uncle Salomon); yet the vigorous healthy primitivism of this young creature must have satisfied a mysterious longing of his own nature, for he himself was a doomed man. His strange headaches had been an early danger signal. In January 1845 (he had just turned forty-eight) he suffered his first stroke; three years later, a peculiar disease, a progressive muscular atrophy, at that time unidentified, stole upon him, paralyzed his right side, shrank his legs, and closed his left eye so that, in order to write, he had to hold his lid open with his fingers. And write he would, in spite of the horrible agonies of the eight years of his "mattress-tomb," from which he could not rise, agonies which chastened and ennobled his soul and his poetry, and which he suffered with serenity and grim humor. "Dying is something horrible," he remarked, "not death if there be one at all." He returned during these years to a personal God, perhaps because without such a God his suffering would be too senseless and cruel a jest of nature; his old defense reaction of frivolous wit, however, remained alive: "Dieu me pardonnera," he said, "c'est son métier."

The outbreak of Heine's disease forms the natural cesura between the two periods of his writings in Paris. In the first, from 1831 to 1843, he assumes the role of interpreter between his native country and that of his adoption. Mostly for the *Augsburger Allgemeine Zeitung*, the first German newspaper of international stature, he writes on French political, social, and cultural life. In these reports he showed himself favorably inclined toward the constitutional monarchy of the bourgeois king, Louis Philippe, though recognizing the danger of an emerging new caste, the financial and industrial plutocracy which threatened to replace the nobility and the clergy as props of the throne. Some day, he hoped, France might readopt a republican form of government, for which Germany, on the other hand, seemed to him politically not mature enough.

For the benefit of the French he published his two long essays, one on the *Romantic School in Germany* in the periodical *L'Europe littéraire* (1833), the other, *Concerning the History of Religion and Philosophy in Germany* in the *Revue des deux Mondes* (1834). In the latter, after a vigorous appraisal of Luther and the German Reformation, Heine harks back to his favorite theme of Hellenism and Nazarenism, which he now treats under the concepts of Pantheism and Deism. By this time Goethe and Herder had infused into Spinoza's static universe the all-pervading dynamic power of an ever creative deity. Heine now adds to it pantheistic elements of the socialistic theories of Saint-Simon (1760-1825) and his followers. They demanded an unlimited production, which would create wealth by and for all, of material as well as spiritual goods. God, being matter as well as spirit, had created body and soul, both equally sacred, as were their products, their work, and their enjoyment. Hence, according to Saint-Simon, the rights of bequest and inheritance should be abolished and every worker should be assured the right to the means of production. All instruments of labor, land, and capital should be united in one social fund, operated on principles of association by hierarchy, so that every individual should have his task according to his capacity, his compensation according to his work. Thus landowners, industrialists, and merchants would become public functionaries in an effectively planned Christian economic society, the political form of which would be unimportant.

What attracted Heine in this peculiar utopian ideal of a state socialism was, no doubt, a recognition of the natural inequality of men, the aristocratic trend of a stratification according to intelligence and spiritual achievement and the so-called emancipation of the flesh, the hallowing of the senses. It seemed to be a solution for the perpetual conflict of European intellectual history, namely that between pagan (Greek) and Judeo-Christian ideals: on the one hand, the affirmation of life in all its aspects and in a harmony of all the human faculties, on the other, the condemnation of the material and sensuous side of existence. This conflict has been a central tradition in German thinking from the middle of the eighteenth century to the present day. We find it presented in many of Heine's later poems, especially in the pantheistic *New Creed* (p. 145) and the mythological condensation of the ideas in *Psyche* (p. 17).

For a while, then, it seemed to Heine that Saint-Simonism could reconcile an abundant life in beauty with a Christian spirit of sympathy with the poor; but serious doubts were soon to assail him in witnessing the degeneration of the New Christianity under the disciples of Saint-Simon. If communism it was to be, then the sober dialectic materialism of Karl Marx, who admired Heine's poetry and influenced him during the forties in Paris, was more convincing though frightening in its consequences. Worst of all was the frugal and stoic republicanism of Ludwig Börne, another German exile in Paris, and his small tradesmen's meetings, with their nauseating tobacco stench. The world of culture, Heine feared, would be destroyed in the onslaught of the raw masses. Their egalitarianism would level the hills and fill the valleys, macadam the countrysides, and kill the nightingales. "Why sing the rose, you aristocrat, sing the potato which feeds the populace," he mocks. And incidentally his poet's head might not fare too well under the labor-stained hands of those ruffians. "Democracy," one of his aphorisms reads, "ushers in the end of literature. Liberty and equality of style! Every one may be permitted to write as poorly as he wishes, but nobody should excel and be allowed to write better." After all, Heine was a poet before anything else, and he castigated his fellow poets for debasing the cause of liberty by writing bad verse about it or for betraying poetry by defending a bad cause in good verse. Thus he always managed to affront both conservatives and radicals, poets and poetasters alike. His *Migratory Rats* are the grimmest indictment of both, democratic Philistines and communists.

When his enemies sought to blunt his stinging pen with the slogan "a talent but no character," he ridiculed them in his mirthful *Atta Troll* (1843), the epic of a dancing bear, who, proudly displaying all traits of the author's radical and reactionary adversaries, comes to grief and shame in his attempts at an art denied to his clumsy nature, being "no talent, but a character." The climax of this work is the superb canto with the voluptuous beauties of the three civilizations, Salome, Diana, and Abunda, a proof triumphant of the poet's genius.

After Heine's second visit to Germany in 1844 his sardonic verse travelogue *Germany, a Winter's Tale* appeared, in which his wit, especially at the end, not only descends to unsavory depths, but also conjures up demonic incarnations of Hegelian thought in between the wittiest criticisms of German foibles and institutions. A sinister figure, for instance, follows the poet through the streets of Cologne, and when cornered reveals himself as the executor of the poet's thoughts:

> An axe was carried in ancient Rome
> Preceding the Consul, but mind you,
> You too have a Lictor, although the axe
> Is carried right behind you.
>
> I am your Lictor and follow you
> Unfalteringly with the blinking
> Judicial axe because I am
> The action born of your thinking.
>
> And even though years may pass between,
> I feel no satisfaction
> Till I've changed your thought to reality;
> You think—my task is action.

The *New Poems,* written since 1827 and published in the same volume, are partly symbolic expressions of his political philosophy, clad in simple form and everyday language, studiously avoiding the high-flown and lofty style of the genre used by other poets; here also we find a considerable number of tersely written ballads, stern in tone, leading over to the sombre and sorrow-laden world of the poetry of his last ten years. Their rich harvest is gathered in three collections. *Romancero* (1851), *Poems of 1853 and 1854,* and the posthumously published *Last Poems and Meditations* (1869). In bulk they are about equal to the two former books;

"Lamentations," the title of one of their sections, is descriptive of well-nigh all of them, even of their ballads. Characteristic is their tendency toward understatement, for instance when Heine calls himself "unyoung and not quite healthy" while he is almost sixty and a desperately sick man, or when he uses a foreign word instead of the German expression which would carry with it too strong an emotion.

In the macabre tragedy of these poems death is the *ultima ratio regis*. Death stands at every door where life is at its highest—of king, of prima donna, of poet. The Asra die when love befalls them. Why all this suffering? ask the songs grouped under the portentous title "Lazarus." Is God not almighty? Is he making sport of us? The only answer we receive is the mouthful of earth. It were better not to have been born, he exclaims in the words of Sophocles. Heine, the supreme lover of life, even on his death bed, becomes his double, watching the slow decomposition of his body with an acute and alert mind. Time "snailing" its hours is the constant subject of his verses. He lives on only to write about dying though he yearns for oblivion through the waters of Lethe, the river of the netherworld. But still the stern conscience of his craft bids him cast his suffering into restrained verse of heart-rending power. Thus he rises beyond his own stature to measure up to the majesty and grandeur of the grim reaper, his gentle savior.

INHOLT

CONTENTS

HEINRICH HEINE

DIE SCHÖPFUNG

Warum ich eigentlich erschuf
Die Welt, ich will es gern bekennen:
Ich fühlte in der Seele brennen,
Wie Flammenwahnsinn, den Beruf.

Krankheit ist wohl der letzte Grund
Des ganzen Schöpferdrangs gewesen;
Erschaffend konnte ich genesen,
Erschaffend wurde ich gesund.

THE CREATION

The real cause for the creation
Of this my world, I will confess,
Was deep within me a distress,
Like flaming madness, my vocation.

So it appears: disease was then
The cause for that creative urge,
Creating was a fiery purge,
Creating I grew well again.

I
BALLADEN
BALLADS

BELSAZAR

Die Mitternacht zog näher schon;
In stummer Ruh lag Babylon.

Nur oben in des Königs Schloß,
Da flackert's, da lärmt des Königs Troß.

Dort oben in dem Königssaal
Belsazar hielt sein Königsmahl.

Die Knechte saßen in schimmernden Reihn
Und leerten die Becher mit funkelndem Wein.

Es klirrten die Becher, es jauchzten die Knecht;
So klang es dem störrigen Könige recht.

Des Königs Wangen leuchten Glut;
Im Wein erwuchs ihm kecker Mut.

Und blindlings reißt der Mut ihn fort;
Und er lästert die Gottheit mit sündigem Wort.

Und er brüstet sich frech und lästert wild!
Die Knechtenschar ihm Beifall brüllt.

Der König rief mit stolzem Blick;
Der Diener eilt und kehrt zurück.

Er trug viel gülden Gerät auf dem Haupt;
Das war aus dem Tempel Jehovahs geraubt.

Und der König ergriff mit frevler Hand
Einen heiligen Becher, gefüllt bis am Rand.

Und leert ihn hastig bis auf den Grund,
Und rufet laut mit schäumendem Mund:

„Jehovah! Dir künd ich auf ewig Hohn—
Ich bin der König von Babylon!"

BELSHAZZAR

Midnight was slowly coming on;
In silent rest lay Babylon.

But above, in the palace of the King
The torches blazed to the goblets' ring.

There in the royal banquet hall
Belshazzar held his festival.

His vassals in many a glittering line
Emptied their goblets of sparkling wine.

The goblets clinked to the satraps' cheer;
Music it was for the stubborn King's ear.

The blood flamed in his cheeks and eyes;
In the wine he felt his boldness rise.

And, by his blind defiance beguiled,
The God-head with sinful words he defiled.

And to slander he added swaggering boast,
Applauded and cheered by the servile host.

The King commanded with haughty glance,
The servant ran and returned at once,

On his head he carried vessels of gold
From Jehova's temple, sacred and old.

And the King seized from it a holy cup
With wanton hand and filled it up,

And emptied it with a breathless draft
And with foam on his mouth he shouted and laughed:

"Jehovah, I challenge your tottering throne—
I am the King of Babylon!"

Doch kaum das grause Wort verklang,
Dem König ward's heimlich im Busen bang.

Das gellende Lachen verstummte zumal;
Es wurde leichenstill im Saal.

Und sieh! und sieh! an weißer Wand,
Da kam's hervor wie Menschenhand;

Und schrieb, und schrieb an weißer Wand
Buchstaben von Feuer, und schrieb und schwand.

Der König stieren Blicks da saß,
Mit schlotternden Knien und totenblaß.

Die Knechtenschar saß kalt durchgraut,
Und saß gar still, gab keinen Laut.

Die Magier kamen, doch keiner verstand
Zu deuten die Flammenschrift an der Wand.

Belsazar ward aber in selbiger Nacht
Von seinen Knechten umgebracht.

RHAMPSENIT

Als der König Rhampsenit
Eintrat in die goldne Halle
Seiner Tochter, lachte diese,
Lachten ihre Zofen alle.

Auch die Schwarzen, die Eunuchen,
Stimmten lachend ein, es lachten
Selbst die Mumien, selbst die Sphinxe,
Daß sie schier zu bersten dachten.

No sooner the gruesome words were said,
The King's heart secretly filled with dread.

The yelling laughter died in a pall;
And silence of death subdued the hall.

Behold, behold! there at the wall
A human hand was seen by all

That wrote and wrote on the chalk-white stone
Letters of fire, and wrote and was gone,

The King with deathlike face sat there,
With trembling knees and a glassy stare.

The servile horde sat horror-bound,
Aghast and cold, without a sound.

The Magi came, but none at all
Could interpret the flaming writ on the wall.

Belshazzar, however, was put to the sword
In the selfsame night by his servile horde.

RHAMPSENIT

Just as Rhampsenit, the King,
Entered in the golden hall
Of his daughter, she was laughing,
Laughing with her maidens all.

And the blackamoors, the eunuchs
Joined the laughter, even mummies
Laughed, there laughed the silent sphinxes
Till they almost burst their tummies.

Die Prinzessin sprach: „Ich glaubte
Schon den Schatzdieb zu erfassen,
Der hat aber einen toten
Arm in meiner Hand gelassen.

„Jetzt begreif ich, wie der Schatzdieb
Dringt in deine Schatzhauskammern,
Und die Schätze dir entwendet
Trotz den Schlössern, Riegeln, Klammern.

„Einen Zauberschlüssel hat er,
Der erschließet allerorten
Jede Türe, widerstehen
Können nicht die stärksten Pforten.

„Ich bin keine starke Pforte
Und ich hab nicht widerstanden,
Schätze hütend diese Nacht
Kam ein Schätzlein mir abhanden."

So sprach lachend die Prinzessin,
Und sie tänzelt' im Gemache,
Und die Zofen, die Eunuchen
Hoben wieder ihre Lache.

An demselben Tag ganz Memphis
Lachte, selbst die Krokodile
Reckten lachend ihre Häupter
Aus dem schlammig gelben Nile,

Als sie Trommelschlag vernahmen
Und sie hörten an dem Ufer
Folgendes Reskript verlesen
Von dem Kanzelei-Ausrufer:

„Rhampsenit, von Gottes Gnaden
König zu und in Ägypten,
Wir entbieten Gruß und Freundschaft
Unsern Vielgetreun und Liebden.

Spoke the princess: "I was certain
I had caught the treasure thief,
But a dead man's arm he left me,
I discovered to my grief.

"I can see now, how this rascal
Penetrates your vaults of treasures
And can rob you, notwithstanding
Locks and bars and safety measures.

"For a magic key he owns,
And no simple door of mortals
Can resist him, no resistance
Offer him the strongest portals.

"I am no such sturdy portal,
Yielded to that cunning wight,
I, while guarding the King's treasure,
Lost a jewel myself last night."

Thus spoke laughingly the princess,
Skipping, tripping through the hall,
And anew joined in the merry
Laughter maidens, eunuchs all.

On the selfsame day all Memphis
Laughed, and every crocodile
Raised its head in merry laughter
From the slimy yellow Nile,

When they heard a sudden drumming
Near the shore beyond the mire
And this mandate promulgated
By the Royal Chancery crier:

"Rampsenit, by grace of God
King in Egypt and King of it,
We send friendly greetings to Our
Subjects loyal and beloved,

„In der Nacht vom dritten zu dem
Vierten Junius des Jahres
Dreizehnhundert vier und zwanzig
Vor Christi Geburt, da war es,

„Daß ein Dieb aus Unserm Schatzhaus
Eine Menge von Juwelen
Uns entwendet; es gelang ihm
Uns auch später zu bestehlen.

„Zur Ermittelung des Täters
Ließen schlafen Wir die Tochter
Bei den Schätzen—doch auch jene
Zu bestehlen schlau vermocht' er.

„Um zu steuern solchem Diebstahl
Und zu gleicher Zeit dem Diebe
Unsre Sympathie zu zeigen,
Unsre Ehrfucht, Unsre Liebe,

„Wollen Wir ihm zur Gemahlin
Unsre einz'ge Tochter geben
Und ihn auch als Thronnachfolger
In den Fürstenstand erheben.

„Sintemal Uns die Adresse
Unsres Eidams noch zur Stunde
Unbekannt, soll dies Reskript ihm
Bringen Unsrer Gnade Kunde.

„So geschehn den dritten Jenner
Dreizehnhundert zwanzig sechs
Vor Christi Geburt.—Signieret
Von Uns: Rhampsenitus Rex."

Rhampsenit hat Wort gehalten,
Nahm den Dieb zum Schwiegersohne.
Und nach seinem Tode erbte
Auch der Dieb Ägyptens Krone.

10

"And make known that from Our treasure,
June the third to fourth at night
Thirteen hundred four and twenty
B.C., cunningly some wight,

"Up to date still undiscovered,
Many jewels did succeed
In abstracting and, still later,
In repeating such a deed.

"When We had Our daughter sleep there
To detect the bold deceiver,
He not only took more jewels,
Even worse, he did be-thieve her.

"Counteracting further thieving
And concurrently to brief
Our respect and sympathetic
Love for such a master thief,

"We shall raise him to a princedom
And shall wed to him Our own
Royal daughter, designating
Him successor to Our throne.

"Inasmuch as We don't know our
Son-in-law's correct address,
This decree is to apprise him
Of Our high and royal grace.

"On the third of January,
Thirteen hundred twenty-six
B.C.—Signed with Our own royal
Hand, We Rhampsenitus Rex."

Rhampsenit did keep his promise,
Gave the thief his daughter's hand,
And the thief became her father's
Legal heir to crown and land.

11

Er regierte wie die andern,
Schützte Handel und Talente;
Wenig, heißt es, ward gestohlen
Unter seinem Regimente.

DAS GOLDNE KALB

Doppelflöten, Hörner, Geigen
Spielen auf zum Götzenreigen,
Und es tanzen Jakobs Töchter
Um das goldne Kalb herum—
Brumm—brumm—brumm—
Paukenschläge und Gelächter!

Hochgeschürzt bis zu den Lenden
Und sich fassend an den Händen,
Jungfraun edelster Geschlechter
Kreisen wie ein Wirbelwind
Um das Rind—
Paukenschläge und Gelächter!

Aron selbst wird fortgezogen
Von des Tanzes Wahnsinnwogen,
Und er selbst, der Glaubenswächter,
Tanzt im Hohenpriesterrock
Wie ein Bock—
Paukenschläge und Gelächter!

KÖNIG DAVID

Lächelnd scheidet der Despot,
Denn er weiß, nach seinem Tod
Wechselt Willkür nur die Hände,
Und die Knechtschaft hat kein Ende.

He ruled like his predecessors:
Commerce, talents he sustained;
Little stealing is reported
In his realm while he reigned.

THE GOLDEN CALF

Fiddles, flutes and horns fiddydle,
Reverence the golden idol;
Jacob's daughters sing and prance
To the beat of kettle drum,
Brum, brum, brum
Round the calf in boisterous dance.

Arch-aristocratic virgins
Lift their skirts like bawdy urchins,
Baring thighs and clasping hands,
Furiously with flying locks
Round the ox
To the drumbeat join the dance.

Even Aaron grips the fury
Of his tarantelling Jewry;
He, the holy faith-enhancer,
Jumps with flying high priest frock
Like a buck
To the drums, a boisterous prancer.

KING DAVID

Smilingly the despot dies,
Knowing that with his demise
Power only changes hands
And that serfdom never ends.

Armes Volk! wie Pferd' und Farrn
Bleibt es angeschirrt am Karrn,
Und der Nacken wird gebrochen,
Der sich nicht bequemt den Jochen.

Sterbend spricht zu Salomo
König David: „Apropos,
Daß ich Joab dir empfehle,
Einen meiner Generäle.

„Dieser tapfre General
Ist seit Jahren mir fatal,
Doch ich wagte den Verhaßten
Niemals ernstlich anzutasten.

„Du, mein Sohn, bist fromm und klug,
Gottesfürchtig, stark genug,
Und es wird dir leicht gelingen,
Jenen Joab umzubringen."

DIE HEILIGEN DREI KÖNIGE

Die Heil'gen Drei Könige aus Morgenland,
Sie frugen in jedem Städtchen:
„Wo geht der Weg nach Bethlehem,
Ihr lieben Buben und Mädchen?"

Die Jungen und Alten, sie wußten es nicht,
Die Könige zogen weiter;
Sie folgten einem goldenen Stern,
Der leuchtete lieblich und heiter.

Der Stern blieb stehn über Josephs Haus,
Da sind sie hineingegangen;
Das Öchslein brüllte, das Kindlein schrie,
Die Heil'gen Drei Könige sangen.

14

Ah, poor people! To the plow
Hitched they stay like horse and cow,
For the despot always broke
Necks that tried to shun the yoke.

Ere he dies, to Salomo
Speaks King David: "A propos,
Captain Joab, son, I must
Leave in your sagacious trust.

"Many years I have been sore
At this captain, bold and hoar,
Yet, I've never to this day
Dared to let my hate hold sway.

"You, my son, are pious, young,
Wise, godfearing—but you're strong,
And in time you can afford
To put Joab to the sword."

THE HOLY THREE KINGS

The Holy Three Kings from the Orient
Asked all the laddies and lassies:
"We are on our way to Bethlehem;
Could you tell us where the path is?"

The young and the old, they knew it not,
The Kings they searched so keenly;
They followed a lovely golden star,
It lighted their way serenely.

The star stood still over Joseph's house,
There they decided on staying;
The little ox lowed, the little child cried,
The Kings began singing and praying.

DER ASRA

Täglich ging die wunderschöne
Sultanstochter auf und nieder
Um die Abendzeit am Springbrunn,
Wo die weißen Wasser plätschern.

Täglich stand der junge Sklave
Um die Abendzeit am Springbrunn,
Wo die weißen Wasser plätschern;
Täglich ward er bleich und bleicher.

Eines Abends trat die Fürstin
Auf ihn zu mit raschen Worten:
„Deinen Namen will ich wissen,
Deine Heimat, deine Sippschaft!"

Und der Sklave sprach: „Ich heiße
Mohamet, ich bin aus Jemen,
Und mein Stamm sind jene Asra,
Welche sterben, wenn sie lieben."

PSYCHE

In der Hand die kleine Lampe,
In der Brust die große Glut,
Schleichet Psyche zu dem Lager,
Wo der holde Schläfer ruht.

Sie errötet und sie zittert
Wie sie seine Schönheit sieht—
Der enthüllte Gott der Liebe,
Er erwacht und er entflieht.

Achtzehnhundertjähr'ge Buße!
Und die Ärmste stirbt beinah!
Psyche fastet und kasteit sich,
Weil sie Amorn nackend sah.

THE ASRA

Daily went the Sultan's beauteous
Daughter walking for her pleasure
In the evening at the fountain
Where the splashing waters whiten.

Daily stood the youthful bondsman
In the evening at the fountain
Where the splashing waters whiten,
Daily he grew pale and paler.

Then one evening stepped the princess
Up to him with sudden questions:
"You must tell me what your name is,
What your country is, your kinfolk."

And the bondsman said: "Mohamet
Is my name, I am from Yemen,
And my kinsmen are the Asra,
They who die when love befalls them."

PSYCHE

In her hand the little lantern,
Love's great ardor in her breast,
Psyche steals back to the bedside,
Sees the lovely sleeper rest.

And she blushes and she trembles
As his beauteous form she sees,
The revealèd god of lovers
He awakens and he flees.

Eighteen hundred years of penance!
Psyche, pining in distress,
Castigates herself for seeing
Amor in his nakedness.

UNTERWELT

1

„Blieb ich doch ein Junggeselle!"—
Seufzet Pluto tausendmal—
„Jetzt, in meiner Ehstandsqual,
Merk ich, früher ohne Weib
War die Hölle keine Hölle.

„Blieb ich doch ein Junggeselle!—
Seit ich Proserpinen hab,
Wünsch ich täglich mich ins Grab!
Wenn sie keift, so hör ich kaum
Meines Cerberus Gebelle.

„Stets vergeblich, stets nach Frieden
Ring ich. Hier im Schattenreich
Kein Verdammter ist mir gleich!
Ich beneide Sisyphus
Und die edlen Danaiden."

2

Auf goldenem Stuhl, im Reiche der Schatten
Zur Seite des königlichen Gatten,
Sitzt Proserpine
Mit finstrer Miene,
Und im Herzen seufzet sie traurig:

„Ich lechze nach Rosen, nach Sangesergüssen
Der Nachtigall, nach Sonnenküssen—
Und hier unter bleichen
Lemuren und Leichen
Mein junges Leben vertraur ich!

NETHERWORLD

1

"I should have remained unmarried,"
Many times poor Pluto sighed,
"Since I carried home my bride,
I have learned: without a wife
Hell was not yet Hell nor harried.

"Bachelor life was joy and glamor!
Since I Proserpina wed,
I wish daily I were dead!
When she brawls, I scarcely hear
Even Cerberus' yelp and clamor.

"Vainly do I in my quarters
Seek for peace; I'd gladly trade
Punishment with every shade!
I must envy Sisyphus
And King Danaos' proud daughters."

2

On a golden chair, in the realm of the dead,
With the King of Shades to whom she was wed
Sits Proserpeen
With a sombre mien
And her heart feels lorn and weary.

"I yearn for roses, for songs and fun,
For the nightingale and the kiss of the sun,
And here among dour
Pale shade and lemur
My young life is tearful and dreary.

„Bin festgeschmiedet am Ehejoche
In diesem verwünschten Rattenloche!
Und des Nachts die Gespenster,
Sie schaun mir ins Fenster,
Und der Styx, er murmelt so schaurig!

„Heut hab ich den Charon zu Tisch geladen—
Glatzköpfig ist er und ohne Waden—
Auch die Totenrichter,
Langweil'ge Gesichter—
In solcher Gesellschaft versaur ich."

3

Während solcherlei Beschwerde
In der Unterwelt sich häuft,
Jammert Ceres auf der Erde.
Die verrückte Göttin läuft,
Ohne Haube, ohne Kragen,
Schlotterbusig durch das Land,
Deklamierend jene Klagen,
Die euch allen wohlbekannt:

„Ist der holde Lenz erschienen?
Hat die Erde sich verjüngt?
Die besonnten Hügel grünen,
Und des Eises Rinde springt.
Aus der Ströme blauem Spiegel
Lacht der unbewölkte Zeus,
Milder wehen Zephirs Flügel,
Augen treibt das junge Reis.
In dem Hain erwachen Lieder,
Und die Oreade spricht:
‚Deine Blumen kehren wieder,
Deine Tochter kehret nicht!'

"The fettered wife of a royal mole,
I sit in this confounded rat-hole,
And at night the dead
Peep in my bed,
And the Styx murmurs so eery.

"Today I had Charon as dinner guest
(No calves on his legs and no hair on his crest)
And the judges of Hades
(What amusement for ladies!).
And life gets ever more dreary."

3

While such manifold vexation
Down in Hades multiplies,
Ceres wails in agitation.
The demented goddess hies
Without kerchief, without collar,
Breasts aflopping, cap askew,
While reciting in her dolor
All those plaints well known to you:

"Is the earth rejuvenated
And has spring returned again?
Sunny hills are liberated,
Icefree is the verdant plain.
In the rivers' mirror, smiling,
Radiates the cloudless sphere,
Under Zephyr's mild beguiling
Budding branches greet the year.
Songs awaken in the bowers;
But the nymph sings at the shore:
'Though returned are all thy flowers,
Thy own daughter comes no more.'

21

„Ach wie lang ist's, daß ich walle
Suchend auf der Erde Flur!
Titan, deine Strahlen alle
Sandt ich nach der teuren Spur!
Keiner hat mir noch verkündet
Von dem lieben Angesicht,
Und der Tag, der alles findet,
Die Verlorne fand er nicht.
Hast du, Zeus, sie mir entrissen?
Hat, von ihrem Reiz gerührt,
Zu des Orkus schwarzen Flüssen
Pluto sie hinabgeführt?

„Wer wird nach dem düstern Strande
Meines Grames Bote sein?
Ewig stößt der Kahn vom Lande,
Doch nur Schatten nimmt er ein.
Jedem sel'gen Aug verschlossen
Bleibt das nächtliche Gefild,
Und solang der Styx geflossen,
Trug er kein lebendig Bild.
Nieder führen tausend Steige,
Keiner führt zum Tag zurück;
Ihre Träne bringt kein Zeuge
Vor der bangen Mutter Blick."

4

Meine Schwiegermutter Ceres!
Laß die Klagen, laß die Bitten!
Dein Verlangen, ich gewähr es—
Habe selbst so viel gelitten!

"Ah, how long 't is that I wander
Seeking o'er the earth's wide face!
Titan, though thy rays from yonder
Have assisted in the chase,
None succeeded in espying
Her beloved countenance,
And the day, the all-descrying,
Sent in vain its searching glance.
Hast thou, Zeus, in hiding left her?
Or has, ravished by her charms,
Pluto wickedly bereft her
Of her mother's loving arms?

"Who will down to Orcus' portals
Be the herald of my woe?
Since the Styx no living mortals
Ever mirrored in its flow,
Charon's barge no earthly being,
None but dismal shadows bore,
Barred to any mortal's seeing
Still remains the desolate shore.
Downward many paths descending
Lead to the eternal night,
But no witness upward wending
Tells me of my daughter's plight."

4

My dear mother-in-law Ceres,
Cease those plaints which you have proffered,
I shall yield to them in fairness
Since I, too, so much have suffered.

Tröste dich, wir wollen ehrlich
Den Besitz der Tochter teilen,
Und sechs Monden soll sie jährlich
Auf der Oberwelt verweilen.

Hilft dir dort an Sommertagen
Bei den Ackerbaugeschäften;
Einen Strohhut wird sie tragen,
Wird auch Blumen daran heften.

Schwärmen wird sie, wenn den Himmel
Überzieht die Abendröte
Und am Bach ein Bauernlümmel
Zärtlich bläst die Hirtenflöte.

Wird sich freun mit Gret' und Hänschen
Bei des Erntefestes Reigen;
Unter Schöpsen, unter Gänschen
Wird sie sich als Löwin zeigen.

Süße Ruh! Ich kann verschnaufen
Hier im Orkus unterdessen!
Punsch mit Lethe will ich saufen,
Um die Gattin zu vergessen.

5

„Zuweilen dünkt es mich, als trübe
Geheime Sehnsucht deinen Blick—
Ich kenn es wohl, dein Mißgeschick:
Verfehltes Leben, verfehlte Liebe!

„Du nickst so traurig! Wiedergeben
Kann ich dir nicht die Jugendzeit—
Unheilbar ist dein Herzeleid:
Verfehlte Liebe, verfehltes Leben!"

Be consoled, your daughter's presence
We shall share, the year dividing;
For six months she may be with you
On the surface world abiding.

She may help in agriculture
In your busy summer hours
And will wear a broad-brimmed straw hat
And will garland it with flowers.

She will at the rosy sunset
Sentimental wax and vocal
While his flute plays at the brookside
Tenderly some village yokel.

Merrily with Hans and Gretel
At the harvest feast she'll dance it
And with billygoats and goslings,
As the lioness, enhance it.

Sweetest peace! I'll catch my breath then
In the Orkus without fretting!
Punch with Lethe will I guzzle,
My beloved spouse forgetting.

5

"Sometimes, it seems, a secret yearning
Speaks from your troubled eyes of late—
Well do I know your hapless fate:
Frustrated life and love, my wife.

"For me there's no way of returning
That youth when you were gay and fair—
Past healing is your heart's despair:
Frustrated love, frustrated life."

RITTER OLAF

1

Vor dem Dome stehn zwei Männer,
Tragen beide rote Röcke,
Und der eine ist der König
Und der Henker ist der andre.

Und zum Henker spricht der König:
„Am Gesang der Pfaffen merk ich,
Daß vollendet schon die Trauung—
Halt bereit dein gutes Richtbeil."

Glockenklang und Orgelrauschen,
Und das Volk strömt aus der Kirche;
Bunter Festzug, in der Mitte
Die geschmückten Neuvermählten.

Leichenblaß und bang und traurig
Schaut die schöne Königstochter;
Keck und heiter schaut Herr Olaf,
Und sein roter Mund, der lächelt.

Und mit lächelnd rotem Munde
Spricht er zu dem finstern König:
„Guten Morgen, Schwiegervater,
Heut ist dir mein Haupt verfallen.

„Sterben soll ich heut—O, laß mich
Nur bis Mitternacht noch leben,
Daß ich meine Hochzeit feire
Mit Bankett und Fackeltänzen.

"Laß mich leben, laß mich leben,
Bis geleert der letzte Becher,
Bis der letzte Tanz getanzt ist—
Laß bis Mitternacht mich leben!"

SIR OLAF

1

At the door of the cathedral
Stand two men in coats of crimson,
One of them the royal despot,
And the other is the hangman.

And the King speaks to the hangman:
"From the clergy's chant I gather
That the ceremony's ended,—
Ready be for execution."

Peal of bells and flood of organ,
And the folk leave the cathedral;
Gay procession, in its center
Garlanded, the newly wedded.

Deadly pale and sad and fearful
Is the beautiful King's daughter,
Bold and gay appears Sir Olaf,
And his mouth is red and smiling.

With his mouth so red and smiling
Speaks Sir Olaf to the despot:
"Ah, good morning, royal father;
Yes, today my head is forfeit.

"Die I must today, but grant me
Ah, that I may live till midnight
And may celebrate my wedding
With a banquet and a torchdance.

"Grant my life, yes grant my life yet
Till I've emptied the last goblet,
Till the last dance I have treaded,
Grant to let me live till midnight."

Und zum Henker spricht der König:
„Unserm Eidam sei gefristet
Bis um Mitternacht sein Leben—
Halt bereit dein gutes Richtbeil."

2

Herr Olaf sitzt beim Hochzeitschmaus,
Er trinkt den letzten Becher aus.
An seine Schulter lehnt
Sein Weib und stöhnt—
Der Henker steht vor der Türe.

Der Reigen beginnt, und Herr Olaf erfaßt
Sein junges Weib, und mit wilder Hast
Sie tanzen, bei Fackelglanz,
Den letzten Tanz—
Der Henker steht vor der Türe.

Die Geigen geben so lustigen Klang,
Die Flöten seufzen so traurig und bang!
Wer die beiden tanzen sieht,
Dem erbebt das Gemüt—
Der Henker steht vor der Türe.

Und wie sie tanzen, im dröhnenden Saal,
Herr Olaf flüstert zu seinem Gemahl:
„Du weißt nicht, wie lieb ich dich hab—
So kalt ist das Grab—"
Der Henker steht vor der Türe.

3

Herr Olaf, es ist Mitternacht,
Dein Leben ist verflossen!
Du hattest eines Fürstenkinds
In freier Lust genossen.

And the King speaks to the hangman:
"To our son-in-law be granted
And vouchsafed his life till midnight;
With your good axe then be ready."

2

Sir Olaf sits in the wedding hall.
He drains his cup and orders the ball
While his moaning young bride
Leans on his side—
The hangman stands at the portal.

The dance begins, he holds enlaced
His bride as they dance in furious haste,
They dance in the torchlight's trance
His final dance—
The hangman stands at the portal.

The fiddles sing so merry and glad,
The sigh of the flutes is so fearful and sad;
And trembling averts his glance
Who sees them dance—
The hangman stands at the portal.

In the din of the hall, in his frenzied stride
Sir Olaf whispers to his bride:
"My love is truer than gold—
The grave so cold—"
The hangman stands at the portal.

3

Sir Olaf, the midnight bell has tolled,
Your life is wellnigh over;
You've lusted after the King's own child
You've been her unblessed lover.

Die Mönche murmeln das Totengebet,
Der Mann im roten Rocke,
Er steht mit seinem blanken Beil
Schon vor dem schwarzen Blocke.

Herr Olaf steigt in den Hof hinab,
Da blinken viel Schwerter und Lichter.
Es lächelt des Ritters roter Mund,
Mit lächelndem Munde spricht er:

„Ich segne die Sonne, ich segne den Mond
Und die Stern', die am Himmel schweifen.
Ich segne auch die Vögelein,
Die in den Lüften pfeifen.

„Ich segne das Meer, ich segne das Land
Und die Blumen auf der Aue.
Ich segne die Veilchen, sie sind so sanft
Wie die Augen meiner Fraue.

„Ihr Veilchenaugen meiner Frau,
Durch euch verlier ich mein Leben!
Ich segne auch den Holunderbaum,
Wo du dich mir ergeben."

BERTRAND DE BORN

Ein edler Stolz in allen Zügen,
Auf seiner Stirn Gedankenspur,
Er konnte jedes Herz besiegen,
Bertrand de Born, der Troubadour.

Es kirrten seine süßen Töne
Die Löwin des Plantagenets;
Die Tochter auch, die beiden Söhne,
Er sang sie alle in sein Netz.

The monks murmur the funeral prayers;
The man in the crimson mantle
On the black block rests his shining axe
And leans upon its handle.

Sir Olaf down to the courtyard goes
'Mongst swords in the torchlight procession;
A smile is on the knight's red lips
And smiling his lips make profession:

"I bless the sun, I bless the moon
And the stars through the heavens swinging.
I also bless the little birds
That sweeten the air with singing.

"I bless the sea, I bless the land
And the flowers that bloom in the shady
Valley where the violets grow,
So blue as the eyes of my lady.

"You violet eyes of my lady love,
Through you my life is over!
I also bless the lilac tree
Where you yielded yourself to your lover."

BERTRAND DE BORN

A noble pride in every feature,
His temples with the thinker's lure,
He won the heart of every creature,
Bertrand de Born, the troubadour.

The magic of his verses vanquished
The wife of the Plantagenet
And both his sons; the daughter languished;
He sang them all into his net.

Wie er den Vater selbst betörte!
In Tränen schmolz des Königs Zorn,
Als er ihn lieblich reden hörte,
Den Troubadour, Bertrand de Born.

BALLADE

Es war ein alter König,
Sein Herz war schwer, sein Haupt war grau;
Der arme alte König,
Er nahm eine junge Frau.

Es war ein schöner Page,
Blond war sein Haupt, leicht war sein Sinn;
Er trug die seidne Schleppe
·Der jungen Königin.

Kennst du das alte Liedchen?
Es klingt so süß, es klingt so trüb!
Sie mußten beide sterben,
Sie hatten sich viel zu lieb.

DIE GRENADIERE

Nach Frankreich zogen zwei Grenadier',
Die waren in Rußland gefangen.
Und als sie kamen ins deutsche Quartier,
Sie ließen die Köpfe hangen.

Da hörten sie beide die traurige Mär:
Daß Frankreich verloren gegangen,
Besiegt und zerschlagen das große Heer—
Und der Kaiser, der Kaiser gefangen.

So also was their father's faring,
In tears dissolved his wrath and scorn
Before the honey-tongued ensnaring
Of troubadour Bertrand de Born.

BALLAD

There was an aged monarch,
His heart was sad and gray his hair;
The poor old king, he married
A lady young and fair.

There was a handsome page boy,
Blond was his hair, gay was his mien;
't was he who carried the silken
Train of his fair young queen.

The old song—you recall it—
It sounds so sweet, it sounds so sad,
It was their fate to perish,
Too great was the love they had.

THE GRENADIERS

Toward France came walking two grenadiers,
They had been captives in Russia.
They hung their heads in shame and tears
When they reached quarters in Prussia;

For there they heard the woeful fate
That the power of France was shaken,
Vanquished the army, once so great—
And the Emperor, the Emperor taken.

Da weinten zusammen die Grenadier'
Wohl ob der kläglichen Kunde.
Der eine sprach: „Wie weh wird mir,
Wie brennt meine alte Wunde!"

Der andre sprach: „Das Lied ist aus,
Auch ich möcht mit dir sterben,
Doch hab ich Weib und Kind zu Haus,
Die ohne mich verderben."

„Was schert mich Weib, was schert mich Kind,
Ich trage weit beßres Verlangen;
Laß sie betteln gehn, wenn sie hungrig sind—
Mein Kaiser, mein Kaiser gefangen!

„Gewähr mir, Bruder, eine Bitt':
Wenn ich jetzt sterben werde,
So nimm meine Leiche nach Frankreich mit,
Begrab mich in Frankreichs Erde.

„Das Ehrenkreuz am roten Band
Sollst du aufs Herz mir legen;
Die Flinte gib mir in die Hand,
Und gürt mir um den Degen.

„So will ich liegen und horchen still
Wie eine Schildwach im Grabe,
Bis einst ich höre Kanonengebrüll
Und wiehernder Rosse Getrabe.

„Dann reitet mein Kaiser wohl über mein Grab,
Viel Schwerter klirren und blitzen;
Dann steig ich gewaffnet hervor aus dem Grab—
Den Kaiser, den Kaiser zu schützen!"

Then wept together the grenadiers
At the doleful news they were learning;
The one said: "Brother, what cause for tears!
Oh, how my old wound is burning!"

The other spoke: "Done is the dance!
My own life I don't cherish,
But I've a wife and child in France
Who without me will perish."

"What matters wife and child to me
When our honor is lost and forsaken?
Let them go beg if they hungry be—
My Emperor, my Emperor taken.

"When I now die, grant one request,
Which, brother keeps me worried,
Oh, take my body along, in the bless'd
French soil I want to be buried.

"Lay the Legion's cross with crimson band
On my heart—do grant this favor!
And put the musket in my hand
And gird me with my saber.

"Thus shall I harken for evermore,
A sentry of our French forces,
Until I hear the cannons roar
And the neighing of galloping horses.

"Then rides my Emperor over my grave,
Our swords gunflashes reflecting,
Then shall I rise full-armed from the grave—
The Emperor, the Emperor protecting."

DAS SKLAVENSCHIFF

Der Superkargo Mynheer van Koek
Sitzt rechnend in seiner Kajüte;
Er kalkuliert der Ladung Betrag
Und die probablen Profite.

„Der Gummi ist gut, der Pfeffer ist gut,
Dreihundert Säcke und Fässer;
Ich habe Goldstaub und Elfenbein—
Die schwarze Ware ist besser.

„Sechshundert Neger tauschte ich ein
Spottwohlfeil am Senegalflusse.
Das Fleisch ist hart, die Sehnen sind stramm,
Wie Eisen vom besten Gusse.

„Ich hab zum Tausche Branntewein,
Glasperlen und Stahlzeug gegeben;
Gewinne daran achthundert Prozent,
Bleibt mir die Hälfte am Leben.

„Bleiben mir Neger dreihundert nur
Im Hafen von Rio Janeiro,
Zahlt dort mir hundert Dukaten per Stück
Das Haus Gonzales Perreiro.“

Da plötzlich wird Mynheer van Koek
Aus seinen Gedanken gerissen;
Der Schiffschirurgus tritt herein,
Der Doktor van der Smissen.

Das ist eine klapperdürre Figur,
Die Nase voll roter Warzen—
„Nun Wasserfeldscherer,“ ruft von Koek,
„Wie geht's meinen lieben Schwarzen?“

THE SLAVESHIP

The supercargo Mynheer van Koek
Sits in his cabin accounting,
He calculates the possible gains
And sees his profits mounting.

"The rubber is good, the pepper is good,
Three hundred barrels and cases;
I have also golddust and ivory
And blacks of excellent races.

"Six hundred negroes I traded for,
Dirtcheap, at the Senegal river;
Their flesh is firm, their muscles tough
Like iron, the best they deliver.

"Brandy I gave in exchange for them,
Cutlery, beads and headware,
I'll clear a pretty eight hundred percent
If only half of them get there.

"And if I've only three hundred left
When landing at Rio Janeiro,
A hundred ducats per head they'll pay,
At the house of Gonzales Pereiro."

While thus the thoughts of Mynheer van Koek
Are on his profits converging,
This matter of business is rudely disturbed
By Doctor van Smissen, the surgeon.

That man has a body thin as a rail,
His nose full of warts and pimples—
"Well, seafaring sawbones," cries van Koek,
"How are my dear black simples?"

Der Doktor dankt der Nachfrage und spricht:
„Ich bin zu melden gekommen,
Daß heute Nacht die Sterblichkeit
Bedeutend zugenommen.

„Im Durchschnitt starben täglich zwei,
Doch heute starben sieben,
Vier Männer, drei Frauen—Ich hab den Verlust
Sogleich in die Kladde geschrieben.

"Ich inspizierte die Leichen genau;
Denn diese Schelme stellen
Sich manchmal tot, damit man sie
Hinabwirft in die Wellen.

„Ich nahm den Toten die Eisen ab;
Und wie ich gewöhnlich tue,
Ich ließ die Leichen werfen ins Meer
Des Morgens in der Fruhe.

„Es schossen alsbald hervor aus der Flut
Haifische, ganze Heere,
Sie lieben so sehr das Negerfleisch;
Sie sind meine Pensionäre.

„Sie folgten unseres Schiffes Spur,
Seit wir verlassen die Küste;
Die Bestien wittern den Leichengeruch
Mit schnupperndem Fraßgelüste.

„Es ist possierlich anzusehn,
Wie sie nach den Toten schnappen!
Die faßt den Kopf, die faßt das Bein,
Die andern schlucken die Lappen.

„Ist alles verschlungen, dann tummeln sie sich
Vergnügt um des Schiffes Planken
Und glotzen mich an, als wollten sie
Sich für das Frühstück bedanken."

"Thanks for the concern," the doctor replies,
"What I report is unnerving;
Since last night their mortality
Has started an upward curving.

"The average death is two per day;
However, today it's seven.
My log this morning records: four males,
Three females have gone to heaven.

"I made an inspection, for I had found
These rascals develop a notion
Of faking death in order to be
Thrown out into the ocean.

"I took off their irons from hand and foot;
And, as it is my custom,
Early at sunrise some of the crew
Over the railing thrust 'em.

"At once there shot out schools of sharks
As if obeying orders;
They're very fond of nigger flesh,
That's why I call them my boarders.

"They've followed in the wake of the ship
Ever since we're en route, Sir;
These beasts can smell the scent of a stiff
For miles and wait for the loot, Sir.

"It's really funny to see them snap
At a corpse with their dentured hinges;
One grasps the head, one takes the leg
And the others swallow the fringes.

"When everything's downed, they merrily play
Around with careening pranks, Sir,
And grin at me as if for the lunch
They wanted to say: many thanks, Sir."

Doch seufzend fällt ihm in die Red'
Van Koek: „Wie kann ich lindern
Das Übel? wie kann ich die Progression
Der Sterblichkeit verhindern?"

Der Doktor erwidert: „Durch eigne Schuld
Sind viele Schwarze gestorben;
Ihr schlechter Odem hat die Luft
Im Schiffsraum so sehr verdorben.

„Auch starben viele durch Melancholie,
Dieweil sie sich tötlich langweilen;
Durch etwas Luft, Musik und Tanz
Läßt sich die Krankheit heilen."

Da ruft van Koek: „Ein guter Rat!
Mein teurer Wasserfeldscherer
Ist klug wie Aristoteles,
Des Alexanders Lehrer.

„Der Präsident der Sozietät
Der Tulpenveredlung in Delfte
Ist sehr gescheit, doch hat er nicht
Von eurem Verstande die Hälfte.

„Musik! Musik! Die Schwarzen solln
Hier auf dem Verdecke tanzen.
Und wer sich beim Hopsen nicht amüsiert,
Den soll die Peitsche kuranzen."

2

Hoch aus dem blauen Himmelszelt
Viel tausend Sterne schauen,
Sehnsüchtig glänzend, groß und klug,
Wie die Augen von schönen Frauen.

But, sighing, interrupted his talk
Van Koek: "This 's got to be finished;
Progression of such mortality
Must by all means be diminished."

The Doctor replies: "It's their own fault!
Due to the vitiation
Of the air in the hold by their stinking breath
They die of asphixiation.

"Also by melancholia
And boredom they're expedited,
But maybe with a little fresh air
And music and dance we can fight it."

"Yes," cries van Koek, "that's sound advice;
My medical staff commander
Is wise like Aristotle, by Jove,
The teacher of Alexander.

"Doctor, the clever President
Of the Dutch Association
For Tulip Improvement has not one half
Your power of observation.

"Music, music will keep these blacks
On the ship's deck hopping and skipping;
Whoever will not amuse himself
Will get a thorough whipping."

2

High from the heaven's great blue vault
The stars, in glimmering motion
Like beauteous women's yearning eyes
Gaze down upon the ocean.

Sie blicken hinunter in das Meer,
Das weithin überzogen
Mit phosphorstrahlendem Purpurduft;
Wollüstig girren die Wogen.

Kein Segel flattert am Sklavenschiff,
Es liegt wie abgetakelt;
Doch schimmern Laternen auf dem Verdeck,
Wo Tanzmusik spektakelt.

Die Fiedel streicht der Steuermann,
Der Koch, der spielt die Flöte,
Der Schiffsjung schlägt die Trommel dazu,
Der Doktor bläst die Trompete.

Wohl hundert Neger, Männer und Fraun,
Sie jauchzen und hopsen und kreisen
Wie toll herum; bei jedem Sprung
Taktmäßig klirren die Eisen.

Sie stampfen den Boden mit tobender Lust,
Und manche schwarze Schöne
Umschlingt wollüstig den nackten Genoß—
Dazwischen ächzende Töne.

Der Büttel ist Maître des plaisiers,
Und hat mit Peitschenhieben
Die lässigen Tänzer stimuliert,
Zum Frohsinn angetrieben.

Und Dideldumdei und Schnedderedeng!
Der Lärm lockt aus den Tiefen
Die Ungetüme der Wasserwelt,
Die dort blödsinnig schliefen.

Schlaftrunken kommen geschwommen heran
Haifische, viele hundert;
Sie glotzen nach dem Schiff hinauf,
Sie sind verdutzt, verwundert.

They gaze upon the crimson hue
Of the phosphorescent expansion,
Where the waves roll in a lazy swell
And cluck in voluptuous scansion

No sail flaps on the slaveship's mast,
The vessel rides at anchor;
The lanterns shimmer upon the deck
And there is music and clangor.

The helmsman plays the violin,
The cabinboy some drumlet,
The cook's flute merrily doodles and squeaks,
The doctor blows the trumpet.

Some hundred negroes, women and men,
They yell and hop in mad pleasure
Like drunks or insane; at every jump
The irons beat the measure.

They stamp the planks in rapturous glee,
Many a beauty hugs groaning
Her naked partner voluptuously—
Mixed in are plaints of moaning.

For the mate is maître de plaisir,
His whip provides stimulation
For laggard dancers and drives them on
To join the jollification.

And doodledidoo and schnedderedeng—
From the lowest depth of the ocean,
Where they slept in stupor, the monsters rise
Allured by the commotion.

Drowsy with sleep the sharks approach
In schools of many hundred;
They gape up at the shimmering deck,
Dully bemused and bewondered.

Sie merken, daß die Frühstückstund
Noch nicht gekommen und gähnen,
Aufsperrend den Rachen; die Kiefer sind
Bepflanzt mit Sägezähnen.

Und Dideldumdei und Schnedderedeng—
Es nehmen kein Ende die Tänze.
Die Haifische beißen vor Ungeduld
Sich selber in die Schwänze.

Ich glaube, sie lieben nicht die Musik,
Wie viele von ihrem Gelichter,
Trau keiner Bestie, die nicht liebt
Musik! sagt Albions großer Dichter.

Und Schnedderedeng und Dideldumdei—
Die Tänze nehmen kein Ende.
Am Fockmast steht Mynheer van Koek
Und faltet betend die Hände.

„Um Christi willen verschone, o Herr,
Das Leben der schwarzen Sünder!
Erzürnten sie dich, so weißt du ja,
Sie sind so dumm wie die Rinder.

„Verschone ihr Leben um Christi will'n,
Der für uns alle gestorben!
Denn bleiben mir nicht dreihundert Stück,
So ist mein Geschäft verdorben."

EIN WEIB

Sie hatten sich beide so herzlich lieb,
Spitzbübin war sie, er war ein Dieb.
Wenn er Schelmenstreiche machte,
Sie warf sich aufs Bett und lachte.

They see that it is not quite time
For breakfast, open yawning
Their sawteethed maws, and lie in wait
Until the day be dawning.

And doodledidoo and schnedderedeng—
No end of jollifications;
The sharks are bored by the delay
And bite their own tails with impatience.

They don't like music, it seems to me,
Like many beasts of craven
And brutal nature. "Don't trust such brutes,"
Says the poet of Stratford-on-Avon.

And schnedderedeng and doodledidoo—
No end of swirling and swaying;
At the foremast stands Mynheer van Koek
And folds his hands in praying:

"For Jesus' sake, oh spare, good Lord,
The lives of these lads and lasses;
If they've offended, oh Lord, you know
They are just as stupid as asses.

"Oh spare their lives, for Jesus' sake,
Who died for our human salvation.
Unless there remain three hundred head
It spoils my calculation."

A WOMAN

They loved each other beyond belief,
She was a hellcat and he a thief,
He practiced his tricks and thereafter
She rolled on her bed with laughter.

Der Tag verging in Freud und Lust,
Des Nachts lag sie an seiner Brust.
Als man ins Gefängnis ihn brachte,
Sie stand am Fenster und lachte.

Er ließ ihr sagen: „O komm zu mir,
Ich sehne mich so sehr nach dir,
Ich rufe nach dir, ich schmachte—"
Sie warf sich aufs Bett und lachte.

Um sechse des Morgens ward er gehenkt,
Um sieben ward er ins Grab gesenkt;
Sie aber schon um achte
Trank roten Wein und lachte.

LORELEI

Ich weiß nicht, was soll es bedeuten,
Daß ich so traurig bin;
Ein Märchen aus alten Zeiten,
Das kommt mir nicht aus dem Sinn.

Die Luft ist kühl und es dunkelt,
Und ruhig fließt der Rhein;
Der Gipfel des Berges funkelt
Im Abendsonnenschein.

Die schönste Jungfrau sitzet
Dort oben wunderbar,
Ihr goldnes Geschmeide blitzet,
Sie kämmt ihr goldenes Haar.

Sie kämmt es mit goldenem Kamme,
Und singt ein Lied dabei;
Das hat eine wundersame,
Gewaltige Melodei.

They passed their days in joy and jest,
At night she lay close to his breast.
They took him to jail, thereafter
She stood at the window with laughter.

He sent her word: "Oh come to me,
It's only you I want to see—
Whatever may happen thereafter—"
She shook her head with laughter.

They strung him up in the morning at six,
At seven they shoveled him in the ditch;
But already at eight she quaffed her
Red wine and shook with laughter.

LORELEY

I do not know what haunts me,
What saddened my mind all day;
An age-old tale confounds me,
A spell I cannot allay.

The air is cool and in twilight
The Rhine's dark waters flow;
The peak of the mountain in highlight
Reflects the evening glow.

There sits a lovely maiden
Above, so wondrous fair,
With shining jewels laden,
She combs her golden hair.

It falls through her comb in a shower,
And over the valley rings
A song of mysterious power
That lovely maiden sings.

Den Schiffer im kleinen Schiffe
Ergreift es mit wildem Weh;
Er schaut nicht die Felsenriffe,
Er schaut nur hinauf in die Höh.

Ich glaube, die Wellen verschlingen
Am Ende Schiffer und Kahn;
Und das hat mit ihrem Singen
Die Lorelei getan.

IM PFARRHAUS

Der bleiche, herbstliche Halbmond
Lugt aus den Wolken heraus;
Ganz einsam liegt auf dem Kirchhof
Das stille Pfarrerhaus.

Die Mutter liest in der Bibel,
Der Sohn, der starret ins Licht,
Schlaftrunken dehnt sich die ältre,
Die jüngere Tochter spricht:

„Ach Gott, wie einem die Tage
Langweilig hier vergehn!
Nur wenn sie einen begraben,
Bekommen wir etwas zu sehn."

Die Mutter spricht zwischen dem Lesen:
„Du irrst, es starben nur vier,
Seit man deinen Vater begraben,
Dort an der Kirchhofstür."

Die ältre Tochter gähnet:
„Ich will nicht verhungern bei euch,
Ich gehe morgen zum Grafen,
Und der ist verliebt und reich."

The boatman in his small skiff is
Seized by turbulent love,
No longer he marks where the cliff is,
He looks to the mountain above.

I think the waves must fling him
Against the reefs nearby,
And that did with her singing
The lovely Loreley.

AT THE PARSONAGE

The bleak autumnal half-moon
Peers out of the cloudy skies;
All alone in the churchyard
The quiet parsonage lies.

The mother reads the Bible,
The son stares into the light,
Sleepily stretches one daughter,
The younger says full of spite:

"Oh Lord! one day like another,
The same monotonous pace;
Except when they bury a person
Nothing goes on in this place."

The mother looks up from her reading:
"You're wrong, there died but four
After they buried your father
Out there at the churchyard door."

The elder daughter says yawning:
"I will not starve with you,
I 'll go to the Count to-morrow,
He's rich and in love with me too."

Der Sohn bricht aus in Lachen:
„Drei Jäger zechen im Stern,
Die machen Gold und lehren
Mir das Geheimnis gern."

Die Mutter wirft ihm die Bibel
Ins magre Gesicht hinein:
„So willst du, Gottverfluchter,
Ein Straßenräuber sein!"

Sie hören pochen ans Fenster,
Und sehn eine winkende Hand;
Der tote Vater steht draußen
Im schwarzen Pred'gergewand.

SCHLECHTES WETTER

Das ist ein schlechtes Wetter,
Es regnet und stürmt und schneit;
Ich sitze am Fenster und schaue
Hinaus in die Dunkelheit.

Da schimmert ein einsames Lichtchen,
Das wandelt langsam fort;
Ein Mütterchen mit dem Laternchen
Wankt über die Straße dort.

Ich glaube, Mehl und Eier
Und Butter kaufte sie ein;
Sie will einen Kuchen backen
Für's große Töchterlein

Die liegt zu Hause im Lehnstuhl
Und blinzelt schläfrig ins Licht;
Die goldenen Locken wallen
Über das süße Gesicht.

Her brother bursts out laughing:
"Three hunters carouse at the Star;
They can make gold and will teach me
What their tricks and secrets are."

The mother throws her Bible
Into his haggard face:
"Then you want to be a robber
In God's and man's disgrace?"

They hear a knock at the window,
They see a beckoning hand—
In his black preacher's cassock
See the dead father stand.

BAD WEATHER

What miserable weather
With rain and storm and snow;
I sit at the window, looking
Into the darkness below.

There moves a lonely shimmer
Slowly along the street;
With a lantern a little old mother
Toddles on unsure feet.

I think she bought eggs and flour
And butter; she wants to bake
Tonight for her grown-up daughter,
Her darling, another cake.

The daughter sprawls in a rocker
And sleepily squints at the light,
Her sweet young face is surrounded
By her gold locks, curly and bright.

TRAGÖDIE

1

Entflieh mit mir und sei mein Weib,
Und ruh an meinem Herzen aus;
Fern in der Fremde sei mein Herz
Dein Vaterland und Vaterhaus.

Gehst du nicht mit, so sterb ich hier
Und du bist einsam und allein;
Und bleibst du auch im Vaterhaus,
Wirst doch wie in der Fremde sein.

2

(Dieses ist ein wirkliches Volkslied,
welches ich am Rheine gehört.)
Es fiel ein Reif in der Frühlingsnacht,
Er fiel auf die zarten Blaublümelein,
Sie sind verwelket, verdorret.

Ein Jüngling hatte ein Mädchen lieb,
Sie flohen heimlich von Hause fort,
Es wußt weder Vater noch Mutter.

Sie sind gewandert hin und her,
Sie haben gehabt weder Glück noch Stern,
Sie sind verdorben, gestorben.

3

Auf ihrem Grab da steht eine Linde,
Drin pfeifen die Vögel und Abendwinde,
Und drunter sitzt, auf dem grünen Platz,
Der Müllersknecht mit seinem Schatz.

Die Winde die wehen so lind und so schaurig,
Die Vögel die singen so süß und so traurig,
Die schwatzenden Buhlen, die werden stumm,
Sie weinen und wissen selbst nicht warum.

TRAGEDY

1

Come, flee with me and be my wife,
Lay on my heart your head to rest,
Your fatherland and home shall be
Henceforth within your lover's breast.

If you stay here, then I must die
And you are lonely and forlorn,
A stranger you would ever be,
Even in the house where you were born.

2

(This is a real folksong
I heard at the Rhine)

There fell a frost in the night of spring,
It fell on the tender blossoms young
And they are withered and faded.

A lad once loved a maiden fair,
They fled in secret from house and home,
They told neither father nor mother.

They roamed and wandered here and there,
They had nor luck nor guiding star,
They fell by the wayside and perished.

3

Upon their grave a linden grows,
The birds sing in it, the nightwind blows,
And under it on the round green bench
The mill hand sits with his pretty wench.

The winds, they whisper so soft and eery,
The birds, they sing so sweet and dreary,
The chatting lovers fall silent and sigh,
Of a sudden they weep and don't know why.

II
REISEBILDER
TRAVEL PICTURES

———

BERG-IDYLLE

1

Auf dem Berge steht die Hütte,
Wo der alte Bergmann wohnt;
Dorten rauscht die grüne Tanne,
Und erglänzt der goldne Mond.

In der Hütte steht ein Lehnstuhl,
Ausgeschnitzelt wunderlich,
Der darauf sitzt, der ist glücklich,
Und der Glückliche bin ich!

Auf dem Schemel sitzt die Kleine,
Stützt den Arm auf meinen Schoß;
Äuglein wie zwei blaue Sterne,
Mündlein wie die Purpurros'.

Und die lieben blauen Sterne
Schaun mich an so himmelgroß,
Und sie legt den Lilienfinger
Schalkhaft auf die Purpurros'.

„Nein, es sieht uns nicht die Mutter,
Denn sie spinnt mit großem Fleiß,
Und der Vater spielt die Zither,
Und er singt die alte Weis."

Und die Kleine flüstert leise,
Leise, mit gedämpftem Laut;
Manches wichtige Geheimnis
Hat sie mir schon anvertraut:

„Aber seit die Muhme tot ist,
Können wir ja nicht mehr gehn
Nach dem Schützenhof zu Goslar,
Dorten ist es gar zu schön.

MOUNTAIN IDYL

1

On the mountain stands the cottage
Where the good old miner stays;
Over it the hemlock rustles
And the moon sheds golden rays.

In the cottage stands an armchair,
Strangely carved and leather clad,
He who sits in it is happy,
And I am that happy lad.

On the footstool sits the maiden,
On my knees her arms repose;
Eyes like two blue stars she opens,
And her mouth a crimson rose.

As she looks at me, her eyes are
Round and wide as the blue sky,
And she lays her lily finger
On that rose, a rogue and sly.

"No, my mother does not see us,
For she spins and spins away,
And the father plays the zither,
And he sings his ancient lay."

Thus the little maiden whispers
So that nobody may hear,
Many a weighty little secret
Thus confiding to my ear.

"But since Auntie died, no longer
We go over to the fair
At the shooting lodge in Goslar;
Oh, it is so lovely there.

„Hier dagegen ist es einsam,
Auf der kalten Bergeshöh,
Und des Winters sind wir gänzlich
Wie begraben in dem Schnee.

„Und ich bin ein banges Mädchen,
Und ich fürcht mich wie ein Kind
Vor den bösen Bergesgeistern,
Die des Nachts geschäftig sind."

Plötzlich schweigt die liebe Kleine,
Wie vom eignen Wort erschreckt,
Und sie hat mit beiden Händchen
Ihre Äugelein bedeckt.

Lauter rauscht die Tanne draußen,
Und das Spinnrad schnurrt und brummt,
Und die Zither klingt dazwischen,
Und die alte Weise summt:

„Fürcht dich nicht, du liebes Kindchen,
Vor der bösen Geister Macht;
Tag und Nacht, du liebes Kindchen,
Halten Englein bei dir Wacht!"

2

Tannenbaum, mit grünen Fingern,
Pocht ans niedre Fensterlein,
Und der Mond, der stille Lauscher,
Wirft sein goldnes Licht herein.

Vater, Mutter schnarchen leise
In dem nahen Schlafgemach;
Doch wir beide, selig schwatzend,
Halten uns einander wach.

"On the mountain here it's lonely
And much colder than below,
And especially when in winter
We are buried quite in snow.

"And I'm but a fearsome creature
And grow stiff with childish fright
Of the evil mountain spirits
And their wicked pranks at night."

Suddenly the little darling
Puts her hands over her eyes,
Spirits of her own creation
In her mind begin to rise.

Louder now the hemlock rustles
While the wheel keeps up its drum;
To the tinkling of the zither
We can hear the old man hum:

"Never fear, my own sweet darling
Any evil spirit's might,
Angels guard thee, my sweet darling,
Evermore by day and night."

2

With green fingers taps the hemlock
On the low-set window pane,
And the moon, the silent listener,
Throws inside its golden rain.

Father, mother, lightly snoring,
In the nearby chamber sleep
While we two, in blissful chatter
Happily our vigil keep.

„Daß du gar zu oft gebetet,
Das zu glauben wird mir schwer,
Jenes Zucken deiner Lippen
Kommt wohl nicht vom Beten her.

„Jenes böse, kalte Zucken,
Das erschreckt mich jedesmal,
Doch die dunkle Angst beschwichtigt
Deiner Augen frommer Strahl.

„Auch bezweifl' ich, daß du glaubest,
Was so rechter Glaube heißt,
Glaubst wohl nicht an Gott den Vater,
An den Sohn und Heil'gen Geist?"

Ach, mein Kindchen, schon als Knabe,
Als ich saß auf Mutters Schoß,
Glaubte ich an Gott den Vater,
Der da waltet gut und groß;

Der die schöne Erd erschaffen,
Und die schönen Menschen drauf,
Der den Sonnen, Monden, Sternen
Vorgezeichnet ihren Lauf.

Als ich größer wurde, Kindchen,
Noch viel mehr begriff ich schon,
Ich begriff und ward vernünftig,
Und ich glaub auch an den Sohn;

An den lieben Sohn, der liebend
Uns die Liebe offenbart
Und zum Lohne, wie gebräuchlich,
Von dem Volk gekreuzigt ward.

Jetzo, da ich ausgewachsen,
Viel gelesen, viel gereist,
Schwillt mein Herz, und ganz von Herzen
Glaub ich an den Heil'gen Geist.

"That you've prayed too much, I doubt it
And I wonder," says my fair,
"What has caused that sneering quiver
Round your lips; I'm sure, not prayer.

"Oh, that cold and evil quiver,
Every time it terrifies
My poor heart; yet reassuring
Is the warm look in your eyes.

"And I also doubt that really
You believe in thoughts that lead
To a faith in God the Father,
Son and Holy Ghost,—our creed."

Dearest child, when as a little
Boy I sat on Mother's knee,
I believed in God the Father,
Great and good, whose work we see,

Who the earth with all its beauty,
Beauty, too, in man designed,
Who to sun and moon and planets
Their eternal paths defined.

When I grew a little older
And to reason had begun,
Better still I comprehended
And believed in God the Son.

God, the loving Son, whose gospel
On the power of love relied,
Whom in gratitude the people,
As is common, crucified.

Now that I've matured to manhood,
Read and traveled, now engrossed
Feels my swelling heart a grateful
Credence in the Holy Ghost.

Dieser tat die größten Wunder,
Und viel größre tut er noch;
Er zerbrach die Zwingherrnburgen,
Und zerbrach des Knechtes Joch.

Alte Todeswunden heilt er
Und erneut das alte Recht:
Alle Menschen, gleichgeboren,
Sind ein adliges Geschlecht.

Er verscheucht die bösen Nebel
Und das dunkle Hirngespinst,
Das uns Lieb und Lust verleidet,
Tag und Nacht uns angegrinst.

Tausend Ritter, wohlgewappnet,
Hat der Heil'ge Geist erwählt,
Seinen Willen zu erfüllen,
Und er hat sie mutbeseelt.

Ihre teuren Schwerter blitzen,
Ihre guten Banner wehn!
Ei, du möchtest wohl, mein Kindchen,
Solche stolze Ritter sehn?

Nun, so schau mich an, mein Kindchen,
Küsse mich und schaue dreist;
Denn ich selber bin ein solcher
Ritter von dem Heil'gen Geist.

3

Still versteckt der Mond sich draußen
Hinterm grünen Tannenbaum,
Und im Zimmer unsre Lampe
Flackert matt und leuchtet kaum.

He performed the greatest wonders,
Works still greater ones; he broke
Tyrants' overawing strongholds,
And He burst the bondsman's yoke.

Ancient scars of death removing,
He renews our ancient right:
Men are all born free and equal,
Race of noble mind and might.

He dispels the noxious vapors,
The dark specter, born of fright,
Which has spoiled our love and pleasures,
Grinned at us by day and night.

And the Holy Ghost selected
Thousand knights to serve His will,
Fully armed, endowed with courage
All His wishes to fulfill.

And their blessèd swords will glitter,
Their good banners will unfurl!
You, no doubt, would like to see such
Valiant champions too, my girl.

Look at me and kiss me, darling,
Look and understand me right;
Champion of the Holy Spirit,
I myself am such a knight.

3

Quietly the moon goes hiding
In the hemlock's darkgreen limb,
And the lamp that lights our table
Flickers weakly and grows dim.

Aber meine blauen Sterne
Strahlen auf in hellerm Licht,
Und es glühn die Purpurröslein,
Und das liebe Mädchen spricht:

„Kleines Völkchen, Wichtelmännchen,
Stehlen unser Brot und Speck,
Abends liegt es noch im Kasten,
Und des Morgens ist es weg.

„Kleines Völkchen, unsre Sahne
Nascht es von der Milch und läßt
Unbedeckt die Schüssel stehen,
Und die Katze säuft den Rest.

„Und die Katz ist eine Hexe,
Denn sie schleicht bei Nacht und Sturm
Drüben nach dem Geisterberge,
Nach dem altverfallnen Turm.

„Dort hat einst ein Schloß gestanden,
Voller Lust und Waffenglanz;
Blanke Ritter, Fraun und Knappen
Schwangen sich im Fackeltanz.

„Da verwünschte Schloß und Leute
Eine böse Zauberin;
Nur die Trümmer blieben stehen,
Und die Eulen nisten drin.

„Doch die sel'ge Muhme sagte:
Wenn man spricht das rechte Wort
Nächtlich zu der rechten Stunde
Drüben an dem rechten Ort,

„So verwandeln sich die Trümmer
Wieder in ein helles Schloß,
Und es tanzen wieder lustig
Ritter, Fraun und Knappentroß.

But my two blue stars with brighter
Look begin to radiate,
And the crimson rose is glowing
And I hear my darling maid:

"Little imp folk, fairy goblins
Steal our bacon and our bread,
Late at night it's in the cupboard,
In the morning—not a shred.

"Little imp folk come to pilfer,
From the milk they lick the best
Cream and leave the pot uncovered,
And the cat then laps the rest.

"And the cat must be a sorceress;
For she sneaks in stormy nights
Over to the tower ruin
On the Specter Mountain Heights.

"Once there stood a towering castle,
Full of splendor and romance;
Shining knights and squires and ladies
Turned and bowed in torchlight dance.

"Then a wicked old enchantress
Cursed the castle and its guests;
Only ruins now are standing
Where the owls have built their nests.

"But my dead old Auntie told me:
If you only speak the right
Word just at the proper place there
And the proper hour at night,

"Then back to its ancient splendor
Will the castle change again;
Merrily will dance its ladies,
Knights and squires and all their train.

„Und wer jenes Wort gesprochen,
Dem gehören Schloß und Leut,
Pauken und Trompeten huld'gen
Seiner jungen Herrlichkeit."

Also blühen Märchenbilder
Aus des Mundes Röselein,
Und die Augen gießen drüber
Ihren blauen Sternenschein.

Ihre goldnen Haare wickelt
Mir die Kleine um die Händ,
Gibt den Fingern hübsche Namen,
Lacht und küßt und schweigt am End.

Und im stillen Zimmer alles
Blickt mich an so wohlvertraut;
Tisch und Schrank, mir ist, als hätt ich
Sie schon früher mal geschaut.

Freundlich ernsthaft schwatzt die Wanduhr,
Und die Zither, hörbar kaum,
Fängt von selber an zu klingen,
Und ich sitze wie im Traum.

Jetzo ist die rechte Stunde,
Und es ist der rechte Ort;
Ja, ich glaube, von den Lippen
Gleitet mir das rechte Wort.

Siehst du, Kindchen, wie schon dämmert
Und erbebt die Mitternacht!
Bach und Tannen brausen lauter,
Und der alte Berg erwacht.

Zitherklang und Zwergenlieder
Tönen aus des Berges Spalt,
Und es sprießt, wie 'n toller Frühling,
Draus hervor ein Blumenwald;—

"He who speaks it, owns the castle,
Knights and ladies, squires and tower;
Drums and trumpets will pay homage
To his young and lordly power."

Thus the fairy legends blossom
From that rose, so crimson bright,
And her two blue eyes suffuse them
With a magic starborn light.

And she winds her golden tresses
Round my hands in childlike skill,
Gives my fingers pretty nicknames,
Laughs and kisses and grows still.

In the quiet room all objects
Look at me like friends of yore;
Chest and table, all appear as
If I'd seen them long before.

Friendly, seriously the wallclock
Chatters and, scarce heard, there seem
Unseen hands to play the zither,
And I sit as in a dream.

Now must be the fateful moment,
Place as well as hour of night;
From my lips a word is gliding
And I think the word is right.

See, my child, the day is dawning,
Midnight trembles, fades away!
Louder rustle brook and hemlocks,
The old mountain feels the day.

Sounds of zither, songs of goblins
Echo from the mountain's womb,
And with spring's intoxication
Sprouts a wilderness of bloom;—

Blumen, kühne Wunderblumen,
Blätter, breit und fabelhaft,
Duftig bunt und hastig regsam,
Wie gedrängt von Leidenschaft.

Rosen, wild wie rote Flammen,
Sprühn aus dem Gewühl hervor;
Lilien, wie kristallne Pfeiler,
Schießen himmelhoch empor.

Und die Sterne, groß wie Sonnen,
Schaun herab mit Sehnsuchtsglut;
In der Lilien Riesenkelche
Strömet ihre Strahlenflut.

Doch wir selber, süßes Kindchen,
Sind verwandelt noch viel mehr;
Fackelglanz und Gold und Seide
Schimmern lustig um uns her.

Du, du wurdest zur Prinzessin,
Diese Hütte ward zum Schloß,
Und da jubeln und da tanzen
Ritter, Fraun und Knappentroß.

Aber ich, ich hab erworben
Dich und alles, Schloß und Leut;
Pauken und Trompeten huld'gen
Meiner jungen Herrlichkeit!

LÜNEBURG

Mein Herz, mein Herz ist traurig,
Doch lustig leuchtet der Mai;
Ich stehe, gelehnt an der Linde,
Hoch auf der alten Bastei.

Flowers, bold phantastic flowers,
Leaves, gigantic, sway and surge,
Varicolored, tensely moving,
As impelled by violent urge.

Roses, red and flamelike spraying,
O'er the throng of foliage rise;
Lilies, giant crystal pillars,
Suddenly dart to the skies.

And the stars, immense like sunballs,
Downward send their yearning gaze;
In the giant cups of lilies
Streams their flood of golden rays.

We ourselves, sweet little darling,
Are transfigured even more;
Blaze of torches, gold and silken
Gowns move 'round us on the floor.

For our hut became a castle,
Princess and her royal mate
You and I, and knights and ladies
Bow and dance and jubilate.

It was I who won this splendor:
You, the castle, knighthood's flower;
Drums and trumpets pay their homage
To my young and lordly power.

LUENEBURG

My heart, my heart is dreary
In the merry radiance of May,
I lean against the linden
On the bastion old and gray.

Da drunten fließt der blaue
Stadtgraben in stiller Ruh;
Ein Knabe fährt im Kahne
Und angelt und pfeift dazu.

Jenseits erheben sich freundlich
In winziger, bunter Gestalt
Lusthäuser und Gärten und Menschen
Und Ochsen und Wiesen und Wald.

Die Mädchen bleichen Wäsche
Und springen im Gras herum;
Das Mühlrad stäubt Diamanten,
Ich höre sein fernes Gesumm.

Am alten grauen Turme
Ein Schilderhäuschen steht;
Ein rotgeröckter Bursche
Dort auf und nieder geht.

Er spielt mit seiner Flinte,
Die funkelt im Sonnenrot,
Er präsentiert und schultert—
Ich wollt, er schösse mich tot.

AM MEER

Wir saßen am Fischerhause
Und schauten nach der See;
Die Abendnebel kamen
Und stiegen in die Höh.

Im Leuchtturm wurden die Lichter
Allmählich angesteckt,
Und in der weiten Ferne
Ward noch ein Schiff entdeckt.

Below flows the blue water
Quietly in the moat,
Whistling a tune and fishing
A young lad rows his boat.

Beyond in gayest colors
Some tiny objects stand,
Pavilions and gardens and people,
Woods, oxen and meadow land.

On the greensward maids bleach linen,
Frolic and leap around;
The millwheel scatters diamonds,
I hear its humming sound.

There is the old gray tower,
A sentry box below;
A young red-coated soldier
Is pacing to and fro.

He's playing with his rifle,
Which glints in the sunset's red,
He shoulders and presents it—
I wish he would shoot me dead.

BY THE SEA

We sat by the fisherman's cottage
And looked out on the sea;
The evening mists were rising
And drifting up from the lea.

The lanterns in the lighthouse
Were lighted by and by,
And far out in the distance
We could a ship descry.

Wir sprachen von Sturm und Schiffbruch,
Vom Seemann, und wie er lebt,
Und zwischen Himmel und Wasser
Und Angst und Freude schwebt.

Wir sprachen von fernen Küsten,
Vom Süden und vom Nord,
Und von den seltsamen Völkern
Und seltsamen Sitten dort.

Am Ganges duftet's und leuchtet's,
Und Riesenbäume blühn,
Und schöne, stille Menschen
Vor Lotosblumen knien.

In Lappland sind schmutzige Leute,
Plattköpfig, breitmäulig und klein;
Sie kauern ums Feuer und backen
Sich Fische und quäken und schrein.

Die Mädchen horchten ernsthaft,
Und endlich sprach niemand mehr;
Das Schiff war nicht mehr sichtbar,
Es dunkelte gar zu sehr.

Du schönes Fischermädchen,
Treibe den Kahn ans Land;
Komm zu mir und setze dich nieder,
Wir kosen Hand in Hand.

Leg an mein Herz dein Köpfchen
Und fürchte dich nicht zu sehr;
Vertraust du dich doch sorglos
Täglich dem wilden Meer.

We spoke of storm and shipwreck,
Of the seaman and his employ,
How he hovers twixt heaven and water,
Twixt lifelong fear and joy.

We spoke of distant seacoasts,
Of southern and northern strands,
And of the peculiar people
And customs in foreign lands.

By the Ganges in fragrance and sunlight
There bloom gigantic trees,
And before lotos blossoms
Kneel silent and fair devotees.

In Lappland dirty people,
Flatheaded and broad-mouthed, gawk
And squat at the fires, baking
Their fish, and scream and squawk.

The maidens listened intently,
And all were silent at last;
The ship could no longer be sighted,
The darkness fell all too fast.

———

You lovely fishermaiden,
Bring your boat to land,
Come to me and sit by my side here
Cozily hand in hand.

Place on my heart your head now
And don't be afraid of me
Since daily you trustingly venture
Out on the turbulent sea.

73

Mein Herz gleicht ganz dem Meere,
Hat Sturm und Ebb' und Flut,
Und manche schöne Perle
In seiner Tiefe ruht.

———————

Das Fräulein stand am Meere
Und seufzte lang und bang,
Es rührte sie so sehre
Der Sonnenuntergang.

Mein Fräulein, sei'n Sie munter,
Das ist ein altes Stück;
Hier vorne geht sie unter
Und kehrt von hinten zurück.

———————

Es ragt ins Meer der Runenstein,
Da sitz ich mit meinen Träumen.
Es pfeift der Wind, die Möven schrein,
Die Wellen, die wandern und schäumen.

Ich habe geliebt manch schönes Kind
Und manchen guten Gesellen—
Wo sind sie hin? Es pfeift der Wind,
Es schäumen und wandern die Wellen.

———————

Sie floh vor mir wie'n Reh so scheu,
Und wie ein Reh geschwinde!
Sie kletterte von Klipp zu Klipp,
Ihr Haar das flog im Winde.

My heart is like the ocean,
Has storm and ebb and flow,
And many a pearl of beauty
Lies in its depth below.

The lady stood by the ocean
With many a sigh and tear,
She saw with such emotion
The sunball disappear.

Young lady, why this fretting?
It is a common sight.
In front you see it setting
And rising behind as bright.

The rune stone juts out from the beach,
I sit there, my dreams aroaming;
There whistles the wind, the seagulls screech,
The waves roll wandring and foaming.

I've loved so many a beautiful child
And many a lad while roaming—
Where are they now? The wind blows wild,
The waves roll wandring and foaming.

She fled from me like a doe so shy
And like a doe so fleeting!
She nimbly climbed from cliff to cliff,
Her hair the breezes beating.

Wo sich zum Meer der Felsen senkt,
Da hab ich sie erreichet,
Da hab ich sanft mit sanftem Wort
Ihr sprödes Herz erweichet.

Hier saßen wir so himmelhoch,
Und auch so himmelselig;
Tief unter uns, ins dunkle Meer,
Die Sonne sank allmählich.

Tief unter uns, ins dunkle Meer,
Versank die schöne Sonne;
Die Wogen rauschten drüber hin,
Mit ungestümer Wonne.

O weine nicht, die Sonne liegt
Nicht tot in jenen Fluten;
Sie hat sich in mein Herz versteckt
Mit allen ihren Gluten.

———————

Mit schwarzen Segeln segelt mein Schiff
Wohl über das wilde Meer;
Du weißt, wie sehr ich traurig bin,
Und kränkst mich doch so schwer.

Dein Herz ist treulos wie der Wind
Und flattert hin und her;
Mit schwarzen Segeln segelt mein Schiff
Wohl über das wilde Meer.

———————

Es ziehen die brausenden Wellen
Wohl nach dem Strand;
Sie schwellen und sie zerschellen
Wohl auf dem Sand.

And where the rock falls off to the sea
In my pursuit I reached her
And gently won her vestal heart,
With gentle words beseeched her.

And here we sat so heaven-high
In heavenly emotion;
Deep down below the setting sun
Sank into the dark ocean.

Deep down below the beautiful sun
Sank into the dark ocean,
The roaring waves effaced its path
In turbulent commotion.

Oh do not weep, the sun does not
Lie dead where the waves are churning.
It went to hide deep in my heart,
In all its radiance burning.

———————

With jetblack sails is sailing my ship
Over the heaving sea;
You know how sad with grief I am
And yet you torture me.

Your heart is faithless as the wind
And flutters luff and lee;
With jetblack sails is sailing my ship
Over the heaving sea.

———————

The roaring waves keep rushing
Toward the strand,
They swell and tumble, gushing
Over the sand.

Sie kommen groß und kräftig,
Ohn Unterlaß;
Sie werden endlich heftig—
Was hilft uns das?

DIE NORDSEE

ABENDDÄMMERUNG

Am blassen Meeresstrande
Saß ich gedankenbekümmert und einsam.
Die Sonne neigte sich tiefer und warf
Glührote Streifen anf das Wasser,
Und die weißen, weiten Wellen,
Von der Flut gedrängt,
Schäumten und rauschten näher und näher—
Ein seltsam Geräusch, ein Flüstern und Pfeifen,
Ein Lachen und Murmeln, Seufzen und Sausen,
Dazwischen ein wiegenliedheimliches Singen—
Mir war, als hört ich verschollne Sagen,
Uralte, liebliche Märchen,
Die ich einst, als Knabe,
Von Nachbarskindern vernahm,
Wenn wir am Sommerabend,
Auf den Treppensteinen der Haustür,
Zum stillen Erzählen niederkauerten,
Mit kleinen, horchenden Herzen
Und neugierklugen Augen;—
Während die großen Mädchen,
Neben duftenden Blumentöpfen,
Gegenüber am Fenster saßen,
Rosengesichter,
Lächelnd und mondbeglänzt.

They come and swell unceasing
And never fail,
Their furious roll increasing—
To what avail?

THE NORTH SEA

EVENING TWILIGHT

On the pale sands of the ocean
I sat in troubled thought and lonely.
The sun sank lower and cast
Redglowing streamers upon the water.
And the wide, white waves
At the urge of the tide
Foamed and billowed closer and closer—
The strangest sound: a whispering and whistling,
A laughing and murmuring, sighing and surging,
Mixed with a singing of cradlesong comfort—
It seemed I was hearing forgotten sagas,
Age-old enchanting tales,
Which I once as a boy
Heard from children of neighbors
When of a summer evening
On the stone stoop of the house
We crouched for a quiet hour of stories
With little harkening hearts
And wide expectant eyes;—
While the big girls
Beside fragrant flower pots
Sat at the window across,
Rose-like faces,
Smiling and bright from the moon.

Die Sonnenlichter spielten
Über das weithinrollende Meer;
Fern auf der Reede glänzte das Schiff,
Das mich zur Heimat tragen sollte;
Aber es fehlte an gutem Fahrwind,
Und ich saß noch ruhig auf weißer Düne
Am einsamen Strand,
Und ich las das Lied vom Odysseus,
Das alte, das ewig junge Lied,
Aus dessen meerdurchrauschten Blättern
Mir freudig entgegenstieg
Der Atem der Götter
Und der leuchtende Menschenfrühling
Und der blühende Himmel von Hellas.

Mein edles Herz begleitete treulich
Den Sohn des Laertes in Irrfahrt und
    Drangsal,
Setzte sich mit ihm, seelenbekümmert,
An gastliche Herde,
Wo Königinnen Purpur spinnen,
Und half ihm lügen und glücklich entrinnen
Aus Riesenhöhlen und Nymphenarmen,
Folgte ihm nach in kimmerische Nacht
Und in Sturm und Schiffbruch
Und duldete mit ihm unsägliches Elend.

Seufzend sprach ich: „Du böser Poseidon,
Dein Zorn ist furchtbar,
Und mir selber bangt
Ob der eignen Heimkehr."

POSEIDON

The sunbeams played
Over the wide-billowing sea;
Distant at anchor lay gleaming the ship
That was to carry me homeward;
But we lacked fair wind for the journey,
And I quietly sat still on the white dune
At the lonely shore,
And I read the song of Ulysses,
The old, the ever new song,
Out from whose sea-breathing pages
Rose, joyous to greet me,
The breath of the gods
And the luminous spring of mankind
And the blooming heaven of Hellas.

My noble heart was faithful companion
To the son of Laertes in wandering and
    hardship
And, filled with sadness, sat down beside him
At welcoming hearths
Where queens spin royal purple,
And helped him to tell his lies and to escape
From giant caves and arms of nymphs,
Followed him into Cimmerian night,
Into storm and shipwreck
And suffered with him unending affliction.

Sighing I spoke: "You wicked Poseidon,
Your wrath is dreadful,
And with fear I am filled
For my own returning."

Kaum sprach ich die Worte,
Da schäumte das Meer,
Und aus den weißen Wellen stieg
Das schilfbekränzte Haupt des Meergotts,
Und höhnisch rief er:

„Fürchte dich nicht, Poetlein!
Ich will nicht im geringsten gefährden
Dein armes Schiffchen,
Und nicht dein liebes Leben beängst'gen
Mit allzu bedenklichem Schaukeln.
Denn du, Poetlein, hast nie mich erzürnt,
Du hast mir kein einziges Türmchen verletzt
An Priamos' heiliger Feste,
Kein einziges Härchen hast du versengt
Am Aug meines Sohns Polyphemos,
Und dich hat niemals ratend beschützt
Die Göttin der Klugheit, Pallas Athene."

Also rief Poseidon
Und tauchte zurück ins Meer;
Und über den groben Seemannswitz
Lachten unter dem Wasser
Amphitrite, das plumpe Fischweib,
Und die dummen Töchter des Nereus.

DIE GÖTTER GRIECHENLANDS

Vollblühender Mond! In deinem Licht,
Wie fließendes Gold, erglänzt das Meer;
Wie Tagessklarheit, doch dämmrig verzaubert,
Liegt's über der weiten Strandesfläche;
Und am hellblau, sternenlosen Himmel
Schweben die weißen Wolken,
Wie kolossale Götterbilder
Von leuchtendem Marmor.

Scarce spoke I these words
When up foamed the sea
And from the white waves rose
The reed-crowned head of the seagod,
And scornful he cried:

"Be not afraid, little poet!
I will not endanger the least
Your paltry vessel
And will not frighten your precious life
With all too precarious rocking.
For you, little poet, have never enraged me,
No single turret you damaged
Of Priam's hallowed fortress,
No single hairlet you singed
Of the eye of my son Polyphemos,
And never with counsel she helped to protect you,
The goddess of prudence, Pallas Athena."

Thus cried Poseidon
And plunged back into the sea;
And at this rude joke of a seaman
Laughed under the water
Amphitrite, the clumsy fishwife,
And the stupid daughters of Nereus.

THE GODS OF GREECE

Fullblooming moon! In your light
Like liquid gold sparkles the sea;
Light like the day's, but in milky enchantment,
Lies over the wide expanse of the strand,
And on the light-blue starless sky
Float the white clouds
Like colossal figures of gods
In shimmering marble.

Nein, nimmermehr, das sind keine Wolken!
Das sind sie selber, die Götter von Hellas,
Die einst so freudig die Welt beherrschten,
Doch jetzt, verdrängt und verstorben,
Als ungeheure Gespenster dahinziehn
Am mitternächtlichen Himmel.

Staunend und seltsam geblendet, betracht ich
Das luftige Pantheon,
Die feierlich stummen, graunhaft bewegten
Riesengestalten.
Der dort ist Kronion, der Himmelskönig,
Schneeweiß sind die Locken des Haupts,
Die berühmten, olymposerschütternden Locken.
Er hält in der Hand den erloschenen Blitz,
In seinem Antlitz liegt Unglück und Gram,
Und doch noch immer der alte Stolz.
Das waren bessere Zeiten, o Zeus,
Als du dich himmlisch ergötztest
An Knaben und Nymphen und Hekatomben;
Doch auch die Götter regieren nicht ewig,
Die jungen verdrängen die alten,
Wie du einst selber den greisen Vater
Und deine Titanen-Öhme verdrängt hast,
Jupiter Parricida!
Auch dich erkenn ich, stolze Juno!
Trotz all deiner eifersüchtigen Angst
Hat doch eine andre das Zepter gewonnen,
Und du bist nicht mehr die Himmelskön'gin,
Und dein großes Aug ist erstarrt,
Und deine Lilienarme sind kraftlos,
Und nimmermehr trifft deine Rache
Die gottbefruchtete Jungfrau
Und den wundertätigen Gottessohn.
Auch dich erkenn ich, Pallas Athene!

No, nevermore, these are not clouds,
They are the real, the gods of Hellas,
Who once so joyfully ruled the world,
But now, thrust out and dead,
Pass as gigantic phantoms along
Over the skies at midnight.

Amazed and strangely blinded I behold
The airy pantheon,
The solemnly silent, appallingly moving
Forms of the giants.
There is Kronion, the king of heaven.
Snowwhite are the locks of his head,
Those famous Olympus-shaking locks.
He holds in his hand the extinguished bolt.
On his countenance lie misfortune and grief,
And yet, as of old, the ancient pride.
Those were happier times, oh Zeus,
When you took a heavenly pleasure
In boys and nymphs and hekatombs;
But even the gods do not rule forever,
The young dislodge the old
As once yourself dislodged your aged father
And your uncles, the Titans,
Jupiter Parricida!
You too I discern, proud Juno!
In spite of all your jealous fear
Another woman usurped the scepter
And you are no longer the queen of heaven.
And your large eye froze to a stare
And your lily-arms are enfeebled
And nevermore will your vengefulness strike
The God-visited Virgin
And the miracle-working Son of the Lord.
You too I discern, Pallas Athena!

Mit Schild und Weisheit konntest du nicht
Abwehren das Götterverderben?
Auch dich erkenn ich, auch dich, Aphrodite,
Einst die goldene, jetzt die silberne!
Zwar schmückt dich noch immer des Gürtels Liebreiz,
Doch graut mir heimlich vor deiner Schönheit,
Und wollt mich beglücken dein gütiger Leib,
Wie andre Helden, ich stürbe vor Angst—
Als Leichengöttin erscheinst du mir,
Venus Libitina!
Nicht mehr mit Liebe blickt nach dir
Dort der schreckliche Ares.

Es schaut so traurig Phöbus Apollo,
Der Jüngling. Es schweigt seine Lei'r,
Die so freudig erklungen beim Göttermahl.
Noch trauriger schaut Hephästos,
Und wahrlich! der Hinkende! nimmermehr
Fällt er Heben ins Amt
Und schenkt geschäftig in der Versammlung
Den lieblichen Nektar.—Und längst ist erloschen
Das unauslöschliche Göttergelächter.

Ich hab euch niemals geliebt, ihr Götter!
Denn widerwärtig sind mir die Griechen,
Und gar die Römer sind mir verhaßt.
Doch heil'ges Erbarmen und schauriges Mitleid
Durchströmt mein Herz,
Wenn ich euch jetzt da droben schaue,
Verlassene Götter,
Tote, nachtwandelnde Schatten,
Nebelschwache, die der Wind verscheucht—
Und wenn ich bedenke, wie feig und windig
Die Götter sind, die euch besiegten,
Die neuen, herrschenden, tristen Götter,
Die schadenfrohen im Schafspelz der Demut—

With shield and wisdom could not even you
Ward off the doom of the gods?
You too I discern, you too, Aphrodite,
Once the golden! Now paled to silver!
Adorned you are still with the charm-lending girdle,
And in secret I dread the sight of your beauty,
And if your generous body would grant me its favors,
As to other heroes, I should die of terror.
A charnel goddess to me you appear,
Venus Libitina!
No longer in love glances at you
Yonder the dreadful Ares.

So sad are the eyes of Phoebus Apollo,
The youthful. His lyre is silent,
Which once so joyfully sang at the feast of the gods.
Still sadder the look of Hephaistos,
And truly, the limpfoot, no longer
Does he assume the service of Hebe
To pour around the assembly
The delicious nectar.—And long is extinguished
The inextinguishable Olympian laughter.

I have never loved you, you gods!
For repulsive to me are the Greeks
And still more hateful to me are the Romans.
But holy compassion and shuddering pity
Stream through my heart
When I behold you yonder,
Forsaken gods,
Dead, somnambulous shadows,
Weak as the mist dispelled by a wind—
And when I consider how cowardly windy
The gods are by whom you were vanquished,
The new, ruling, pitiful gods,
Malicious, in sheepskins of self-abasement,

O, da faßt mich ein düsterer Groll,
Und brechen möcht ich die neuen Tempel,
Und kämpfen für euch, ihr alten Götter,
Für euch und eu'r gutes ambrosisches Recht,
Und vor euren hohen Altären,
Den wiedergebauten, den opferdampfenden,
Möcht ich selber knieen und beten,
Und flehend die Arme erheben—

Denn immerhin, ihr alten Götter
Habt ihr's auch ehmals, in Kämpfen der Menschen
Stets mit der Partei der Sieger gehalten,
So ist doch der Mensch großmüt'ger als ihr,
Und in Götterkämpfen halt ich es jetzt
Mit der Partei der besiegten Götter.

*   *   *

Also sprach ich, und sichtbar erröteten
Droben die blassen Wolkengestalten
Und schauten mich an wie Sterbende,
Schmerzenverklärt, und schwanden plötzlich.

Der Mond verbarg sich eben
Hinter Gewölk, das dunkler heranzog;
Hoch aufrauschte das Meer,
Und siegreich traten hervor am Himmel
Die ewigen Sterne.

FRAGEN

Am Meer, am wüsten, nächtlichen Meer
Steht ein Jüngling-Mann,
Die Brust voll Wehmut, das Haupt voll Zweifel,
Und mit düstern Lippen fragt er die Wogen:

„O löst mir das Rätsel des Lebens,
Das qualvoll uralte Rätsel,
Worüber schon manche Häupter gegrübelt,

Oh, then I am seized by a sullen rancor
And I long to break the newer temples
And battle for you, you ancient gods,
For you and your valid ambrosian rights,
And before your lofty altars,
Re-erected, steaming with offerings,
Would I kneel and pray myself
And lift up my arms beseeching—

For, after all, though you ancient gods
When men were fighting in days of old,
Were ever on the side of the victors,
Man, in truth, is more generous than you,
And in the conflict of gods I now hold
To the side of the gods who are vanquished.

*   *   *

Thus I spoke; visibly flushed
Up yonder the pallid cloud-born shapes
And gazed, as if dying, upon me,
Transfigured by pain, and suddenly vanished.

Just then the moon went into hiding
Behind the clouds which darkly approached;
High up surged the sea
And triumphant emerged in the sky
The stars eternal.

QUESTIONS

By the sea, the desolate, nocturnal sea
Stands a youth-man,
His heart full of sadness, his mind full of doubt,
And with gloomy lips he questions the waves:

"Oh solve for me the riddle of life,
The tormenting age-old riddle,
Over which so many heads have brooded,

Häupter in Hieroglyphenmützen,
Häupter in Turban und schwarzem Barett,
Perückenhäupter und tausend andre
Arme, schwitzende Menschenhäupter—
Sagt mir, was bedeutet der Mensch?
Woher ist er kommen? Wo geht er hin?
Wer wohnt dort oben auf goldenen Sternen?"

Es murmeln die Wogen ihr ew'ges Gemurmel,
Es wehet der Wind, es fliehen die Wolken,
Es blinken die Sterne, gleichgültig und kalt,
Und ein Narr wartet auf Antwort.

IM HAFEN

Glücklich der Mann, der den Hafen erreicht hat
Und hinter sich ließ das Meer und die Stürme,
Und jetzo warm und ruhig sitzt
Im guten Ratskeller zu Bremen.

Wie doch die Welt so traulich und lieblich
Im Römerglas sich widerspiegelt,
Und wie der wogende Mikrokosmos
Sonnig hinabfließt ins durstige Herz!
Alles erblick ich im Glas,
Alte und neue Völkergeschichte,
Türken und Griechen, Hegel und Gans,
Zitronenwälder und Wachtparaden,
Berlin und Schilda und Tunis und Hamburg,
Vor allem aber das Bild der Geliebten,
Das Engelköpfchen auf Rheinweingoldgrund.

O, wie schön! wie schön bist du, Geliebte!
Du bist wie eine Rose!
Nicht wie die Rose von Schiras,
Die hafisbesungene Nachtigallbraut;
Nicht wie die Rose von Saron,

Heads in hieroglyphed cone caps,
Heads in turbans, heads in black barrets,
Heads bewigged and a thousand other
Poor sweating heads of mortals—
Tell me what meaning has man?
Whence has he come? And whither he goes?
Who dwells up yonder on golden stars?"

The waves murmur their eternal murmur,
The wind blows, the clouds pass fleeting,
The stars twinkle, indifferent and cold,
And a fool waits for an answer.

IN PORT

Happy the man who has reached the harbor
And left behind the sea and the tempests
And now sits quiet and warm
In the good Ratskeller of Bremen.

How friendly and lovely the world looks
When mirrored in a green goblet,
And how the surging microcosmos
Radiantly flows into the thirsty heart!
I see it all in the glass:
Old and recent history of man,
Turks and Greeks, Hegel and Gans,
Groves of lemons and change of the guards,
Berlin, Gotham, Tunis and Hamburg,
And above all, the face of my sweetheart,
The angel head on the goldground of Rhinewine.

Oh, how fair! How fair you are, Beloved!
Like a rose you are,
Not like the rose of Shiraz,
The nightingale-bride sung by Hafiz;
Not like the rose of Sharon,

Die heiligrote, prophetengefeierte;—
Du bist wie die Ros' im Ratskeller zu Bremen!
Das ist die Rose der Rosen,
Je älter sie wird, je lieblicher blüht sie,
Und ihr himmlischer Duft, er hat mich beseligt,
Er hat mich begeistert, er hat mich berauscht,
Und hielt mich nicht fest, am Schopfe fest,
Der Ratskellermeister von Bremen,
Ich wäre gepurzelt!

Der brave Mann! Wir saßen beisammen
Und tranken wie Brüder,
Wir sprachen von hohen, heimlichen Dingen,
Wir seufzten und sanken uns in die Arme,
Und er hat mich bekehrt zum Glauben der Liebe—
Ich trank auf das Wohl meiner bittersten Feinde,
Und allen schlechten Poeten vergab ich,
Wie einst mir selber vergeben soll werden,—
Ich weinte vor Andacht, und endlich
Erschlossen sich mir die Pforten des Heils,
Wo die zwölf Apostel, die heil'gen Stückfässer,
Schweigend pred'gen, und doch so verständlich
Für alle Völker.

Das sind Männer!
Unscheinbar von außen, in hölzernen Röcklein,
Sind sie von innen schöner und leuchtender
Denn all die stolzen Leviten des Tempels
Und des Herodes Trabanten und Höflinge,
Die goldgeschmückten, die purpurgekleideten—
Hab ich doch immer gesagt,
Nicht unter ganz gemeinen Leuten,
Nein, in der allerbesten Gesellschaft
Lebte beständig der König des Himmels!

The holy red one, praised by the prophets;—
You are like the Rose in the Ratskeller of Bremen;
That is the rose of roses,
The older it grows, the lovelier it blooms,
And its heavenly fragrance, it delighted my soul,
It filled me with rapture, with intoxication,
And had not held me fast by the forelock
The Ratskeller butler of Bremen,
I should have tumbled!

That honest man! we sat together
And drank like brothers,
We spoke of lofty, mysterious things,
We sighed and sank into each other's arms,
And he converted me to the creed of love,—
I drank to the health of my bitterest enemies
And forgave all measly poets,
As in days to come I shall be forgiven,—
I wept with devotion and lastly
Were opened to me the portals of Grace,
Where the Twelve Apostles, the sacred wine casks,
Silently preach, and yet so clearly
To all peoples.

Those are fellows!
Outwardly simple, in wooden vestments,
They are finer within and more radiant,
Than all the haughty Levites of the Temple
And King Herod's guardsmen and courtiers,
Laden with gold and clad in crimson—
Have I not always said,
Not amongst common people,
No, in the very best of company
Dwelt at all times the King of Heaven!

Halleluja! Wie lieblich umwehn mich
Die Palmen von Beth-El!
Wie duften die Myrrhen von Hebron!
Wie rauscht der Jordan und taumelt vor Freude!—
Auch meine unsterbliche Seele taumelt,
Und ich taumle mit ihr, und taumelnd
Bringt mich die Treppe hinauf, ans Tagslicht,
Der brave Ratskellermeister von Bremen.

Du braver Ratskellermeister von Bremen!
Siehst du, auf den Dächern der Häuser sitzen
Die Engel und sind betrunken und singen;
Die glühende Sonne dort oben
Ist nur eine rote, betrunkene Nase,
Die Nase des Weltgeists;
Und um die rote Weltgeistnase
Dreht sich die ganze, betrunkene Welt.

Hallelujah! How gently they fanned me,
The palm trees of Beth-El!
How fragrant the myrrh of Hebron!
How the Jordan murmurs and tumbles with gladness!
So also staggers my soul, the immortal,
And I stagger with it, and staggering
Leads me up the stairs to daylight
The honest Ratskeller butler of Bremen.

You honest Ratskeller butler of Bremen!
Look, on the roofs of the houses sit
The angels and are drunk and singing;
The glowing sun up yonder
Is naught but a red and drunken nose,
The nose of the Weltgeist,
And around the red Weltgeist nose
Turns the whole drunken world.

III
UNGLÜCKLICHE LIEBE
UNHAPPY LOVE

———

Auf Flügeln des Gesanges,
Herzliebchen, trag ich dich fort,
Fort nach den Fluren des Ganges,
Dort weiß ich den schönsten Ort.

Dort liegt ein rotblühender Garten
Im stillen Mondenschein;
Die Lotosblumen erwarten
Ihr trautes Schwesterlein.

Die Veilchen kichern und kosen
Und schaun nach den Sternen empor;
Heimlich erzählen die Rosen
Sich duftende Märchen ins Ohr.

Es hüpfen herbei und lauschen
Die frommen, klugen Gazell'n;
Und in der Ferne rauschen
Des heiligen Stromes Well'n.

Dort wollen wir niedersinken
Unter dem Palmenbaum
Und Lieb und Ruhe trinken
Und träumen seligen Traum.

———

Die Lotosblume ängstigt
Sich vor der Sonne Pracht,
Und mit gesenktem Haupte
Erwartet sie träumend die Nacht.

Der Mond, der ist ihr Buhle,
Er weckt sie mit seinem Licht,
Und ihm entschleiert sie freundlich
Ihr frommes Blumengesicht.

On wings of song I carry
You far, my love, through the air,
Down at the Ganges we'll tarry,
At a place so fragrant and fair.

A rose-blooming garden will greet you
In quiet moon-lit night;
The lotos are longing to meet you,
Their sister, in loving delight.

The violets titter caressing
And graze to the starry heights;
The roses whisper, confessing
Sweet-scented fairy-tale nights.

There leap to us gently and listen
The tame and wide-eyed gazelles;
And far away murmur and glisten
The holy river's swells.

Under the palm tree sinking,
Shaded from moonlight gleam,
And rest and rapture drinking,
We'll dream a wonderful dream.

———————

The lotus flower is frightened
By the sun's majestic light;
With downcast eyes and dreaming
She longs for the quiet of night.

The moon, he is her lover,
He wakes her with silver rays;
To him she unveils her friendly
Devoted flower face.

Sie blüht und glüht und leuchtet
Und starret stumm in die Höh;
Sie duftet und weinet und zittert
Vor Liebe und Liebesweh.

Ein Fichtenbaum steht einsam
Im Norden auf kahler Höh.
Ihn schläfert; mit weißer Decke
Umhüllen ihn Eis und Schnee.

Er träumt von einer Palme,
Die fern im Morgenland
Einsam und schweigend trauert
Auf brennender Felsenwand.

Ein Jüngling liebt ein Mädchen,
Die hat einen andern erwählt;
Der andre liebt eine andre
Und hat sich mit dieser vermählt.

Das Mädchen heiratet aus Ärger
Den ersten besten Mann,
Der ihr in den Weg gelaufen;
Der Jüngling ist übel dran.

Es ist eine alte Geschichte,
Doch bleibt sie immer neu;
Und wem sie just passieret,
Dem bricht das Herz entzwei.

Ich grolle nicht, und wenn das Herz auch bricht,
Ewig verlornes Lieb! Ich grolle nicht.
Wie du auch strahlst in Diamantenpracht,
Es fällt kein Strahl in deines Herzens Nacht.

She blooms and sparkles, gazing
Silently up to his glow;
In fragrance she weeps and trembles
From rapture of love and woe.

———

A hemlock tree stands lonely
Far north on craggy height.
He drowses; ice and snowfall
Cover him cold and white.

He dreams of a young palm tree,
She, lonely and without hope,
Mourns in the distant Orient
On rocky sun-parched slope.

———

A young man loves a maiden
Whose heart for another sighed;
This other loves another
Who then becomes his bride.

The maiden takes the first man
Who happens to come her way
Just out of spite and anger;
The youth is left in dismay.

It is an old old story
And yet it's always new;
And to whomever it happens
't will break his heart in two.

———

I feel no rancor, though my heart be sore,
Nor spite, beloved, lost for evermore,
For though you glitter in your diamonds' light,
No ray will fall into your heart's dark night.

Das weiß ich längst. Ich sah dich ja im Traum,
Und sah die Nacht in deines Herzens Raum,
Und sah die Schlang, die dir am Herzen frißt,
Ich sah, mein Lieb, wie sehr du elend bist.

Es fällt ein Stern herunter
Aus seiner funkelnden Höh!
Das ist der Stern der Liebe,
Den ich dort fallen seh.

Es fallen vom Apfelbaume
Der Blüten und Blätter viel!
Es kommen die neckenden Lüfte
Und treiben damit ihr Spiel.

Es singt der Schwan im Weiher
Und rudert auf und ab,
Und immer leiser singend
Taucht er ins Flutengrab.

Es ist so still und dunkel!
Verweht ist Blatt und Blüt,
Der Stern ist knisternd zerstoben,
Verklungen das Schwanenlied.

Wenn ich an deinem Hause
Des Morgens vorübergeh,
So freut's mich, du liebe Kleine,
Wenn ich dich am Fenster seh.

Mit deinen schwarzbraunen Augen
Siehst du mich forschend an:
„Wer bist du, und was fehlt dir,
Du fremder, kranker Mann?"

I've known it long: I saw you in my dream.
Into your night no hope will cast a gleam;
I saw the serpent on your heart's blood feed
And saw, my love, the life you're doomed to lead.

———

There falls a star from heaven
Far from its twinkling height!
That is the star of lovers,
I see its sinking light.

There fall many apple blossoms
And leaves from nodding tree!
The winds of spring come blowing
And whirl them with teasing glee.

There sings a swan on the water
And glides on darkling wave,
With softer and softer singing
At last goes down to its grave.

It is so dark and quiet!
The blossoms and leaves are gone,
The star is scattered to ashes,
And hushed the song of the swan.

———

When I pass your house in the morning,
You little one, sweet and fair,
I see you at the window,
And am happy when you are there.

Your darkbrown eyes look always
At me inquiringly:
"What ails you, poor sick stranger?
And pray, who may you be?"

Ich bin ein deutscher Dichter,
Bekannt im deutschen Land;
Nennt man die besten Namen,
So wird auch der meine genannt.

Und was mir fehlt, du Kleine,
Fehlt manchem im deutschen Land;
Nennt man die schlimmsten Schmerzen,
So wird auch der meine genannt.

———————

Still ist die Nacht, es ruhen die Gassen,
In diesem Hause wohnte mein Schatz;
Sie hat schon längst die Stadt verlassen,
Doch steht noch das Haus auf demselben Platz.

Da steht auch ein Mensch und starrt in die Höhe
Und ringt die Hände vor Schmerzensgewalt;
Mir graust es, wenn ich sein Antlitz sehe—
Der Mond zeigt mir meine eigne Gestalt.

Du Doppeltgänger, du bleicher Geselle!
Was äffst du nach mein Liebesleid,
Das mich gequält auf dieser Stelle
So manche Nacht in alter Zeit?

———————

Ich unglücksel'ger Atlas! Eine Welt,
Die ganze Welt der Schmerzen muß ich tragen,
Ich trage Unerträgliches, und brechen
Will mir das Herz im Leibe.

Du stolzes Herz, du hast es ja gewollt!
Du wolltest glücklich sein, unendlich glücklich
Oder unendlich elend, stolzes Herz,
Und jetzo bist du elend.

I am a German poet
In German lands well known;
When all the best names are mentioned,
They also name my own.

And what, my darling, ails me
Is in German lands well known;
When the worst pains are mentioned,
They also name my own.

Still is the night, the streets deserted,
My sweetheart lived in the house I face;
She is gone to whom my thoughts reverted,
But the house still stands in the selfsame place.

And there stands a man and seems to beseech her
And wrings his hands in grief and pain;
I shudder, for in his every feature
The moonlight shows my own self again.

You double of mine, you pallid other!
Why do you mimic my love's wild woe
Which tortured me, your wretched brother,
So many a night here long ago?

I most unfortunate Atlas! For a world,
The entire world of suffering I must carry,
I bear what can't be born, and feel the
Heart in my body breaking.

You haughty heart, you wanted it like this!
You wanted to be happy, infinitely,
Or infinitely wretched, haughty heart,
And now, in truth, are wretched.

Die Jahre kommen und gehen,
Geschlechter steigen ins Grab,
Doch nimmer vergeht die Liebe,
Die ich im Herzen hab.

Nur einmal noch möcht ich dich sehen
Und sinken vor dir aufs Knie,
Und sterbend zu dir sprechen:
„Madame, ich liebe Sie!"

„Hat sie sich denn nie geäußert
Über dein verliebtes Wesen?
Konntest du in ihren Augen
Niemals Gegenliebe lesen?

„Konntest du in ihren Augen
Niemals bis zur Seele dringen?
Und du bist ja sonst kein Esel,
Teurer Freund, in solchen Dingen."

Sie liebten sich beide, doch keiner
Wollt es dem andern gestehn;
Sie sahen sich an so feindlich
Und wollten vor Liebe vergehn.

Sie trennten sich endlich und sahn sich
Nur noch zuweilen im Traum;
Sie waren längst gestorben
Und wußten es selber kaum.

Nun ist es Zeit, daß ich mit Verstand
Mich aller Torheit entled'ge,
Ich hab so lang als ein Komödiant
Mit dir gespielt die Komödie.

The years keep coming and going,
Generations pass to the grave,
But never the love will perish
Which in my heart I have.

Just once more I'd like to see you
And sink upon my knee
And speak to you while dying:
"Madame, ich liebe Sie."

———

"Has she never intimated
That she understood your yearning?
Could you never read an answer
In her eyes, your love returning?

"Looking in those eyes, you never
Reached her soul with all your glances?
You're not known to act, dear fellow,
Like an ass in such romances!"

———

They loved one another, but neither
Was moved what he felt to say;
Like enemies looked at each other
While their hearts were pining away.

They parted at last and sometimes
Still saw each other in dreams;
They had long died, but hardly
Knew it themselves, it seems.

———

It's about time that I got some sense
And returned to sober reason;
I have acted with you in silly pretense
Too long in "the play of the season."

Die prächt'gen Kulissen, sie waren bemalt
Im hochromantischen Stile,
Mein Rittermantel hat goldig gestrahlt,
Ich fühlte die feinsten Gefühle.

Und nun ich mich gar säuberlich
Des tollen Tands entled'ge:
Noch immer elend fühl ich mich,
Als spielt ich noch immer Komödie.

Ach Gott! im Scherz und unbewußt
Sprach ich, was ich gefühlet;
Ich hab mit dem Tod in der eignen Brust
Den sterbenden Fechter gespielet.

———

Als ich auf der Reise zufällig
Der Liebsten Familie fand,
Schwesterchen, Vater und Mutter,
Sie haben mich freudig erkannt.

Sie fragten nach meinem Befinden
Und sagten selber sogleich:
Ich hätte mich gar nicht verändert,
Nur mein Gesicht sei bleich.

Ich fragte nach Muhmen und Basen,
Nach manchem langweil'gen Gesell'n
Und nach dem kleinen Hündchen
Mit seinem sanften Bell'n.

Auch nach der vermählten Geliebten
Fragte ich nebenbei;
Und freundlich gab man zur Antwort,
Daß sie in den Wochen sei.

The scenery, splendid to behold,
Was the peak of romantic fashion,
My knightly cloak just glittered with gold
And I felt the finest passion.

And now that I've doffed the farcical
Flitter, the comedy ending,
I still feel just as miserable
As if we were still pretending.

Oh Lord! I acted as in a jest
From a feeling much truer and greater,
I played with death in my own breast
The dying gladiator.

———————

When I lately met on a journey
My sweetheart's family by chance,
Little sister, father and mother,
They recognized me at once.

They asked how I was at present,
But waited for no detail,
Said I looked just as ever,
Only my face was pale.

I inquired about aunts and cousins
And many a tedious chap,
And about the little doggie
With its gentle little yap.

About my married sweetheart
I asked quite casually,
And their answer was very friendly:
She was in a family way.

Und freundlich gratuliert ich
Und lispelte liebevoll,
Daß man sie von mir recht herzlich
Viel tausendmal grüßen soll.

Schwesterchen rief dazwischen:
Das Hündchen, sanft und klein,
Ist groß und toll geworden
Und ward ertränkt im Rhein.

Die Kleine gleicht der Geliebten,
Besonders, wenn sie lacht;
Sie hat dieselben Augen,
Die mich so elend gemacht.

———

Du bist wie eine Blume,
So hold und schön und rein;
Ich schau dich an, und Wehmut
Schleicht mir ins Herz hinein.

Mir ist, als ob ich die Hände
Aufs Haupt dir legen sollt,
Betend, daß Gott dich erhalte
So rein und schön und hold.

———

Nacht liegt auf den fremden Wegen,
Krankes Herz und müde Glieder;—
Ach, da fließt wie stiller Segen,
Süßer Mond, dein Licht hernieder.

Süßer Mond, mit deinen Strahlen
Scheuchest du das nächt'ge Grauen;
Es zerrinnen meine Qualen,
Und die Augen übertauen.

I spoke my congratulations
And lisped that on my part
They should give her a thousand greetings
And good wishes with all my heart.

Little sister then interrupted:
Doggie, so gentle and fine,
Had grown so, but seized by madness
Had to be drowned in the Rhine.

The little one looks like my sweetheart;
Especially laughing she had
The selfsame eyes that forever
Left me forlorn and sad.

You are just like a flower
So fair and chaste and dear;
Looking at you, sweet sadness
Invades my heart with fear.

I feel I should be folding
My hands upon your hair,
Praying that God may keep you
So dear and chaste and fair.

Night on unknown roads, distressing,
Sick the heart, the limbs so weary;—
Ah—there flows into the eery
Night, oh moon, your quiet blessing.

Oh, sweet moonlight, how you banish
And dispel my night-born fears;
All my bitter torments vanish
And my eyes o'erflow with tears.

111

AN JENNY

Ich bin nun fünfunddreißig Jahr alt,
Und du bist fünfzehnjährig kaum ...
O Jenny, wenn ich dich betrachte,
Erwacht in mir der alte Traum!

Im Jahre achzehnhundert siebzehn
Sah ich ein Mädchen, wunderbar
Dir ähnlich an Gestalt und Wesen,
Auch trug sie ganz wie du das Haar.

Ich geh auf Universitäten,
Sprach ich zu ihr, ich komm zurück
In kurzer Zeit, erwarte meiner.
Sie sprach: „Du bist mein einz'ges Glück."

Drei Jahre schon hatt ich Pandekten
Studiert, als ich am ersten Mai
Zu Göttingen die Nachricht hörte,
Daß meine Braut vermählet sei.

Es war am ersten Mai! Der Frühling
Zog lachend grün durch Feld und Tal,
Die Vögel sangen, und es freute
Sich jeder Wurm im Sonnenstrahl.

Ich aber wurde blaß und kränklich,
Und meine Kräfte nahmen ab;
Der liebe Gott nur kann es wissen,
Was ich des Nachts gelitten hab.

Doch ich genas. Meine Gesundheit
Ist jetzt so stark wie'n Eichenbaum ...
O Jenny, wenn ich dich betrachte,
Erwacht in mir der alte Traum!

TO JENNY

I am just thirty-five at present
And scarcely fifteen years are you—
Oh Jenny dear, when I behold you,
My old dream rises up anew!

It was in eighteenhundred seventeen
I saw a maiden, she was fair,
Like you in character and figure
And just like you she wore her hair.

I leave for academic study,
(I said to her), but soon, I guess,
I shall be back, wait for my coming.
She said: "You are my happiness."

Three years I'd studied jurisprudence
When I received the first of May
In Göttingen the information
That married was my fiancée.

It was the first of May! Spring wandered
Through field and forest green and gay,
Birds sang and every meanest creature
Enjoyed the sun's first warming ray.

But I alone grew pale and sickly
And all my strength was on the wane;
And only God knows how I suffered
Night after night in grief and pain.

But I recovered, and my health is
As strong now as an oaken beam—
Oh Jenny dear, when I behold you,
There reawakens my old dream.

IV

AMOURS
FUGITIVES

———

Wir fuhren allein im dunkeln
Postwagen die ganze Nacht;
Wir ruhten einander am Herzen,
Wir haben gescherzt und gelacht.

Doch als es morgens tagte,
Mein Kind, wie staunten wir!
Denn zwischen uns saß Amor,
Der blinde Passagier.

―――――――

Das weiß Gott, wo sich die tolle
Dirne einquartieret hat;
Fluchend in dem Regenwetter
Lauf ich durch die ganze Stadt.

Bin ich doch von einem Gasthof
Nach dem andern hingerannt,
Und an jeden groben Kellner
Hab ich mich umsonst gewandt.

Da erblick ich sie am Fenster,
Und sie winkt und kichert hell.
Konnt ich wissen, du bewohntest,
Mädchen, solches Prachthotel!

―――――――

In meinen Tagesträumen,
In meinem nächtlichen Wachen,
Stets klingt mir in der Seele
Dein allerliebstes Lachen.

Denkst du noch Montmorencys,
Wie du auf dem Esel rittest
Und von dem hohen Sattel
Hinab in die Disteln glittest?

We rode alone in the darkling
Stagecoach together all night;
My heart lay close to your heart,
And we chatted in mirthful delight.

But when it dawned in the morning,
My child, how surprised we were!
For in between us sat Cupid,
Blind stowaway passenger.

———

Heaven knows where the capricious
Chick has found a room in town;
Cursing in the rain I'm running
Streets and alleys up and down.

All the inns in turn I've hunted,
Have in vain those sullen louts,
Waiters, porters in the taverns
Asked as to her whereabouts.

There—I see her at a window,
Beckoning and giggling—Well,
How could I know, honey, that you
Stopped at such a swank hotel.

———

Daydreams and nightly waking
Do now and ever after
Send through my soul an echo
Of your delightful laughter.

Remember Montmorency?
How you were donkey riding
And always from your saddle
Down in the thistles gliding?

Der Esel blieb ruhig stehen,
Fing an, die Disteln zu fressen—
Dein allerliebstes Lachen
Werde ich nie vergessen.

———

Wenn du mir vorüberwandelst,
Und dein Kleid berührt mich nur,
Jubelt dir mein Herz, und stürmisch
Folgt es deiner schönen Spur.

Dann drehst du dich um, und schaust mich
Mit den großen Augen an,
Und mein Herz ist so erschrocken,
Daß es kaum dir folgen kann.

———

Leise zieht durch mein Gemüt
Liebliches Geläute.
Klinge, kleines Frühlingslied,
Kling hinaus ins Weite.

Kling hinaus, bis an das Haus,
Wo die Blumen sprießen.
Wenn du eine Rose schaust,
Sag, ich lass' sie grüßen.

———

Es haben unsre Herzen
Geschlossen die heil'ge Alliance;
Sie lagen fest aneinander,
Und sie verstanden sich ganz.

Ach, nur die junge Rose,
Die deine Brust geschmückt,
Die arme Bundesgenossin,
Sie wurde fast zerdrückt.

The donkey ate the thistles
And nothing would upset it.—
Oh, your delightful laughter,
I never shall forget it!

———

When you pass me and I'm barely
Grazed by fluttering cape or veil,
Jubilates my heart and sends me
Storming on your fragrant trail.

Then you turn your face, just looking
With your eyes so large and blue,
And my trembling heart is frightened
That it scarce can follow you.

———

Faintly sings a song of spring,
Like a maybell's ringing,
Through my heart and spreads its wings,
Into spring air swinging.

Wing your sound where flowers abound,
To the house afleeting,
When you see a rose around,
Say I send her greetings.

———

To form a holy alliance
Our hearts lately agreed,
They lay in firm embracement
And their unison was complete.

Alas, the sweet young rosebud,
Our pitiable ally,
Which then adorned your bosom,
Was almost smothered thereby.

Wie die Nelken duftig atmen!
Wie die Sterne, ein Gewimmel
Goldner Bienen, ängstlich schimmern
An dem veilchenblauen Himmel!

Aus dem Dunkel der Kastanien
Glänzt das Landhaus, weiß und lüstern,
Und ich hör die Glastür klirren
Und die liebe Stimme flüstern.

Holdes Zittern, süßes Beben,
Furchtsam zärtliches Umschlingen—
Und die jungen Rosen lauschen,
Und die Nachtigallen singen.

———————

Küsse, die man stiehlt im Dunkeln
Und im Dunkeln wiedergibt,
Solche Küsse wie besel'gen
Sie die Seele, wenn sie liebt!

Ahnend und erinnrungssüchtig,
Denkt die Seele sich dabei
Manches von vergangnen Tagen,
Und von Zukunft mancherlei.

Doch das gar zu viele Denken
Ist bedenklich, wenn man küßt;—
Weine lieber, liebe Seele,
Weil das Weinen leichter ist.

———————

Morgens send ich dir die Veilchen,
Die ich früh im Wald gefunden,
Und des Abends bring ich Rosen,
Die ich brach in Dämmerstunden.

How the stars, a swarm of golden
Bees in anxious palpitation
Dot the violet sky, and pungent
Incense breathes the carnation!

From the darkened bound of chestnuts
Shines the manor's lucent glister,
And I hear the glassdoor clinking
And the dear beloved's whisper.

Tender hesitant embracing,
Lovely trembling, sweetest throbbing—
The unfolding roses listen
To the nightingales' deep sobbing.

———————

Kisses which one steals in darkness
And in darkness one returns,
Oh, how blissful are such kisses
When our soul in ardor burns!

Both recalling and divining,
In our soul what interplay!
Memories of past embraces,
Visions of a future day.

Be on guard! Excessive thinking
Does not well with kisses blend;
Rather weep, beloved soul, for
Weeping's easier in the end.

———————

Every morn I send you violets,
Found in woods at early hour,
In the evening I bring roses
Which I broke in dusky bower.

Weißt du, was die hübschen Blumen
Dir Verblümtes sagen möchten?
Treu sein sollst du mir am Tage
Und mich lieben in den Nächten.

———

Sorge nie, daß ich verrate
Meine Liebe vor der Welt,
Wenn mein Mund ob deiner Schönheit
Von Metaphern überquellt.

Unter einem Wald von Blumen
Liegt, in still verborgner Hut,
Jenes glühende Geheimnis,
Jene tief geheime Glut.

Sprühn einmal verdächt'ge Funken
Aus den Rosen—sorge nie!
Diese Welt glaubt nicht an Flammen
Und sie nimmt's für Poesie.

———

Du liegst mir so gern im Arme,
Du liegst mir am Herzen so gern!
Ich bin dein ganzer Himmel,
Du bist mein liebster Stern

Tief unter uns da wimmelt
Das närrische Menschengeschlecht;
Sie schreien und wüten und schelten,
Und haben alle recht.

Sie klingeln mit ihren Kappen
Und zanken ohne Grund;
Mit ihren Kolben schlagen
Sie sich die Köpfe wund.

Do you know what from these flowers
You would hear, their language learning?
Faithful shall you be in daytime
And at night requite my yearning.

———————

Never fear, my metaphoric
Verses would my love disclose
When my heart in admiration
Of your beauty overflows.

Underneath this screen of flowers
Deeply hidden lies below
That well guarded glowing secret,
That well guarded secret glow.

Sparks may sometimes under roses
Scintillate suspiciously;
But the world does not believe such
Flames and thinks them poetry.

———————

You love to lie in my arms, dear,
So near my heart you are;
For you I am all heaven,
You are my dearest star.

Deep down below us, people
Swarm in their foolish plight,
They scream and rage and wrangle,
And each contends he is right.

Each jingles with his fool's cap,
Quarrels without a shred
Of reason, grabs his weapon,
And cracks somebody's head.

Wie glücklich sind wir beide,
Daß wir von ihnen so fern—
Du birgst in deinem Himmel
Das Haupt, mein liebster Stern!

Die holden Wünsche blühen
Und welken wieder ab,
Und blühen und welken wieder—
So geht es bis ans Grab.

Das weiß ich und das vertrübet
Mir alle Lieb und Lust;
Mein Herz ist so klug und witzig
Und verblutet in meiner Brust.

Meinen schönsten Liebesantrag
Suchst du ängstlich zu verneinen;
Frag ich dann, ob das ein Korb sei?
Fängst du plötzlich an zu weinen.

Selten bet ich, drum erhör mich,
Lieber Gott! Hilf dieser Dirne,
Trockne ihre süßen Tränen
Und erleuchte ihr Gehirne.

Hol der Teufel deine Mutter,
Hol der Teufel deinen Vater,
Die so grausam mich verhindert
Dich zu schauen im Theater.

Denn sie saßen da und gaben,
Breitgeputzt, nur seltne Lücken,
Dich im Hintergrund der Loge,
Süßes Liebchen, zu erblicken.

How fortunate for us, dear,
To be removed so far;
Within your heaven you bury
Your head, my dearest star.

———

Our lovely wishes blossom
And die and lose their scent,
And bloom again and wither
And so—unto our end.

All this I know; it shadows
My loving and my zest;
My heart is so shrewd and discerning
While bleeding away in my breast.

———

To my nicest declaration
You reply your love denying;
When I ask: are you in earnest,
Suddenly you take to crying.

Seldom do I pray, hence hear me,
Dear Lord, ease this poor girl's tension,
Dry her sweet tears and illumine
Her deficient comprehension.

———

May the devil take your father,
May the devil take your mother;
At the theater they kept us
Cruelly from seeing each other.

For they sat there, broadly planted
In the box, front row, mon bijou,
All dolled up they sat and left me
Not a gap through which to see you,

125

Und sie saßen da und schauten
Zweier Liebenden Verderben,
Und sie klatschten großen Beifall,
Als sie beide sahen sterben.

———

Der Brief, den du geschrieben,
Er macht mich gar nicht bang;
Du willst mich nicht mehr lieben,
Aber dein Brief ist lang.

Zwölf Seiten, eng und zierlich!
Ein kleines Manuskript!
Man schreibt nicht so ausführlich,
Wenn man den Abschied gibt.

———

Vierundzwanzig Stunden soll ich
Warten auf das höchste Glück,
Das mir blinzelnd süß verkündet
Blinzelnd süß der Seitenblick.

O! die Sprache ist so dürftig
Und das Wort ein plumpes Ding;
Wird es ausgesprochen, flattert
Fort der schöne Schmetterling.

Doch der Blick, der ist unendlich,
Und er macht unendlich weit
Deine Brust, wie einen Himmel
Voll gestirnter Seligkeit.

———

Nicht mal einen einz'gen Kuß
Nach so monatlangem Lieben!
Und so bin ich Allerärmster
Trocknen Munds hier stehn gebliebn.

Sat there, witnessing the ruin
Of two lovers, without crying,
And they heartily applauded
When they saw the lovers dying.

———————

The letter you have written
Does not arouse my fear;
You are no longer smitten—
But your letter is long, my dear.

Twelve pages of close writing,
A veritable tome
With details too inviting
For sending a lover home!

———————

Four and twenty hours of patience
Till supreme delight be nigh
Promised by her sidelong glances
And a winking of her eye!

Oh, our speech is so deficient
And the word inert and wry;
Once pronounced, it quickly flutters
Off, the pretty butterfly.

But a glance, it has no limits,
It expands the hoping breast
To a heavenly space, unending
And with thousand starlights blessed.

———————

Not a single loving kiss
After all these months of wooing!
And I—with an unrequited
Mouth like a poor fool stand rueing.

Einmal kam das Glück mir nah—
Schon konnt ich den Atem spüren—
Doch es flog vorüber—ohne
Mir die Lippen zu berühren.

———

Emma, sage mir die Wahrheit:
Ward ich närrisch durch die Liebe?
Oder ist die Liebe selber
Nur die Folge meiner Narrheit?

Ach! mich quälet, teure Emma,
Außer meiner tollen Liebe,
Außer meiner Liebestollheit,
Obendrein noch dies Dilemma.

———

Schon mit ihren schlimmsten Schatten
Schleicht die böse Nacht heran;
Unsre Seelen, sie ermatten,
Gähnend schauen wir uns an.

Du wirst alt und ich noch älter,
Unser Frühling ist verblüht.
Du wirst kalt und ich noch kälter,
Wie der Winter näher zieht.

Ach, das Ende ist so trübe!
Nach der holden Liebesnot
Kommen Nöte ohne Liebe,
Nach dem Leben kommt der Tod.

———

Ich liebe solche weiße Glieder,
Der zarten Seele schlanke Hülle,
Wildgroße Augen und die Stirne
Umwogt von schwarzer Lockenfülle!

Fortune only once came near;
Scarce its breath was I perceiving
When it hurried past—not even
On my lips an impress leaving.

Help me, Emma, I am hazy—
Is it love that made me foolish?
Is perhaps my love not rather
A result of being crazy?

These torment me, dearest Emma:
Loving folly on the one hand,
Foolish loving on the other,
And withal now this dilemma.

All too soon with shadows leery
Evil night is drawing nigh,
And our souls have grown so weary,
Face to face we yawn and sigh.

You grow old and I still older,
And our spring has lost its prime;
You grow cold and I grow colder—
Soon we know it's wintertime.

Ah, the end is full of sadness!
Upon love's sweet maddening strife
Follow loveless strife and madness,
Death at last comes after life.

I love such white and slender bodies,
For tender souls the fitting shrine,
Such large-wild eyes under a forehead
Where tumbling raven locks entwine.

Du bist so recht die rechte Sorte,
Die ich gesucht in allen Landen;
Auch meinen Wert hat euresgleichen
So recht zu würdigen verstanden.

Du hast an mir den Mann gefunden,
Wie du ihn brauchst. Du wirst mich reichlich
Beglücken mit Gefühl und Küssen,
Und dann verraten, wie gebräuchlich.

———

An deine schneeweiße Schulter
Hab ich mein Haupt gelehnt,
Und heimlich kann ich behorchen,
Wonach dein Herz sich sehnt.

Es blasen die blauen Husaren
Und reiten zum Tor herein,
Und morgen will mich verlassen
Die Herzallerliebste mein.

Und willst du mich morgen verlassen,
So bist du doch heute noch mein,
Und in deinen schönen Armen
Will ich doppelt selig sein.

———

Es blasen die blauen Husaren,
Und reiten zum Tor hinaus;
Da komm ich, Geliebte und bringe
Dir einen Rosenstrauß.

Das war eine wilde Wirtschaft!
Kriegsvolk und Landesplag'!
Sogar in deinem Herzchen
Viel Einquartierung lag.

You are indeed the type of woman
Whom I have sought in every land;
And my own worth, it must be granted,
Your kind could always understand.

You found in me the very lover
You need and whom you will repay
With showers of ardent love and kisses,
And then, as usual, betray.

––––––––––

Upon your snowwhite shoulder
I rest my head once more
And hear your heart betraying
What it is longing for.

The blue hussars ride bugling
Into the city gate;
To-morrow you will desert me
And go to capitulate.

And though you leave me to-morrow,
Today I lean on your breast;
In your white arms, my beauty,
I shall be doubly blessed.

––––––––––

The blue hussars ride bugling
Through the city gate and away;
I come to you, my darling,
And bring you a rose bouquet.

That was some wild commotion:
Requisitions and martial yoke!
Even in your little heart lay
Much billeted soldier folk.

YOLANTE UND MARIE

1

Diese Damen, sie verstehen,
Wie man Dichter ehren muß:
Gaben mir ein Mittagessen,
Mir und meinem Genius.

Ach! die Suppe war vortrefflich,
Und der Wein hat mich erquickt,
Das Geflügel, das war göttlich,
Und der Hase war gespickt.

Sprachen, glaub ich, von der Dichtkunst,
Und ich wurde endlich satt;
Und ich dankte für die Ehre,
Die man mir erwiesen hat.

2

In welche soll ich mich verlieben,
Da beide liebenswürdig sind?
Ein schönes Weib ist noch die Mutter,
Die Tochter ist ein schönes Kind.

Die weißen, unerfahrnen Glieder
Sie sind so rührend anzusehn!
Doch reizend sind geniale Augen,
Die unsre Zärtlichkeit verstehn.

Es gleicht mein Herz dem grauen Freunde,
Der zwischen zwei Gebündel Heu
Nachsinnlich grübelt, welch von beiden
Das allerbeste Futter sei.

3

Die Flaschen sind leer, das Frühstück war gut,
Die Dämchen sind rosig erhitzet;
Sie lüften das Mieder mit Übermut,
Ich glaube, sie sind bespitzet.

YOLANTHE AND MARIE

1

These two ladies know that poets
Must be celebrated thus:
They invited me for dinner,
Poor me and my genius.

Ah, the soup was quite superior
And the wine, indeed, was rare,
Most divine the fowl, moreover,
Nicely larded, too, the hare.

While we spoke, I think, of poems,
I did justice to the food;
For their kindness and the honor
I expressed my gratitude.

2

Which of the two my love shall favor
Since I am half by both beguiled?
A handsome woman still the mother,
The daughter is a handsome child.

The white and inexperienced body
It is so touching, I confess;
But charming, too, are eyes of knowledge
Which understand our tenderness.

My heart is like our gray old brother
Who stands between two bales of hay
And deeply ponders which may better
His choosy appetite allay.

3

The bottles are empty, the luncheon was good,
The ladies are heated and rosy;
They loosen their bodice in mirthful mood,
A little tipsy and dozy.

Die Schulter wie weiß, die Brüstchen wie nett!
Mein Herz erbebet vor Schrecken.
Nun werfen sie lachend sich aufs Bett,
Und hüllen sich ein in die Decken.

Sie ziehen nun gar die Gardinen vor,
Und schnarchen am End um die Wette,
Da steh ich im Zimmer, ein einsamer Tor,
Betrachte verlegen das Bette.

4

Jugend, die mir täglich schwindet,
Wird durch raschen Mut ersetzt,
Und mein kühnrer Arm umwindet
Noch viel schlanke Hüften jetzt.

Tat auch manche sehr erschrocken,
Hat sie doch sich bald gefügt;
Holder Zorn, verschämtes Stocken
Wird von Schmeichelei besiegt.

Doch, wenn ich den Sieg genieße,
Fehlt das Beste mir dabei.
Ist es die verschwundne, süße
Blöde Jugendeselei?

Es geht am End', es ist kein Zweifel,
Der Liebe Glut, sie geht zum Teufel.
Sind wir einmal von ihr befreit,
Beginnt für uns die beßre Zeit,
Das Glück der kühlen Häuslichkeit.
Der Mensch genießet dann die Welt,
Die immer lacht fürs liebe Geld.
Er speist vergnügt sein Leibgericht,
Und in den Nächten wälzt er nicht
Schlaflos sein Haupt, er ruhet warm
In seiner treuen Gattin Arm.

Their shoulders so white, their breastlets well set,
My heart wagtails like a plover;
And laughing they throw themselves on the bed
And wrap themselves with the cover.

Even the curtains they finally pull
And compete in snoring seclusion;
There I stand in the room, a lonesome fool,
And look at the bed in confusion.

4

Quick decision now replaces
Youth, increasingly eclipsed,
But my bolder arm enlaces
Nowadays much slend'rer hips.

Many a one seemed scared and quavering,
In the end she would give in;
Sweet irateness, shamefaced wavering
Flattery can always win.

But I feel something is wanting
In the joy of victory;
Is it the long lost enchanting
Youthful asininity?

This is the end, I know it well,
Love's ardor cools and goes to Hell.
Once it is driven from your heart,
Begins for you the better part:
The happy cool domestic art.
Then you enjoy the world each day,
You like to laugh for what you pay,
You eat in peace your favorite dish;
At night no longer feverish
You toss your head—for safe and warm
You rest in your true spouse's arm.

Geleert hab ich nach Herzenswunsch
Der Liebe Kelch, ganz ausgeleert;
Das ist ein Trank, der uns verzehrt
Wie flammenheißer Kognakpunsch.

Da lob ich mir die laue Wärme
Der Freundschaft: jedes Seelenweh
Stillt sie, erquickend die Gedärme
Wie eine fromme Tasse Tee.

I've emptied to my heart's content
Love's chalice to the final drop;
Like cognac punch it burns you up,
A flaming hot bedevilment.

I rather praise the tepid charming
Of friendship, for it sets you free
From all soul's woe, your bowels warming
Just like a saintly cup of tea.

V
AUFLEHNUNG
REVOLT

ADAM DER ERSTE

Du schicktest mit dem Flammenschwert
Den himmlischen Gendarmen,
Und jagtest mich aus dem Paradies,
Ganz ohne Recht und Erbarmen!

Ich ziehe fort mit meiner Frau
Nach andern Erdenländern;
Doch daß ich genossen des Wissens Frucht,
Das kannst du nicht mehr ändern.

Du kannst nicht ändern, daß ich weiß,
Wie sehr du klein und nichtig,
Und machst du dich auch noch so sehr
Durch Tod und Donnern wichtig.

O Gott! wie erbärmlich ist doch dies
Consilium abeundi!
Das nenne ich einen Magnificus
Der Welt, ein Lumen Mundi!

Vermissen werde ich nimmermehr
Die paradiesischen Räume;
Das war kein wahres Paradies—
Es gab dort verbotene Bäume.

Ich will mein volles Freiheitsrecht!
Find ich die g'ringste Beschränknis,
Verwandelt sich mir das Paradies
In Hölle und Gefängnis.

WARNUNG

Solche Bücher läßt du drucken!
Teurer Freund, du bist verloren!
Willst du Geld und Ehre haben,
Mußt du dich gehörig ducken.

ADAM THE FIRST

You ordered with the flaming sword
The heavenly policeman
And chased me out of paradise
Quite without right and easement.

To other lands my wife and I
Must wander, bowed and beaten;
Yet you can't help it: from the fruit
Of knowledge I have eaten.

Nor can you change it that I know
How small you are and blundering,
However you inflate yourself
With all your death and thundering.

Oh God! how pitiful is this
Consilium abeundi!
And such they call Magnificus
Or else a Lumen Mundi!

Whatever hardship, grief and toil
In other lands be hidden,
I shall not miss your paradise.
With trees that are forbidden.

I want full right of liberty!
For, with the least recision
Of such a right, e'en paradise
Is naught but hell and prison.

WARNING

And such books you dare to print!
Dearest friend, you are a goner!
If you money want and honor,
Knuckle under, take the hint!

Nimmer hätt ich dir geraten,
So zu sprechen zu dem Volke,
So zu sprechen von den Pfaffen
Und von hohen Potentaten!

Teurer Freund, du bist verloren!
Fürsten haben lange Arme,
Pfaffen haben lange Zungen,
Und das Volk hat lange Ohren!

GUTER RAT

Gib ihren wahren Namen immer
In deiner Fabel ihren Helden.
Wagst du es nicht, ergeht's dir schlimmer:
Zu deinem Eselsbilde melden
Sich gleich ein Dutzend graue Toren—
„Das sind ja meine langen Ohren!"
Ruft jeder, „dieses gräßlich grimme
Gebreie ist ja meine Stimme!
Der Esel bin ich! Obgleich nicht genannt,
Erkennt mich doch mein Vaterland,
Mein Vaterland Germania!
Der Esel bin ich! I-ah! I-ah!"—

Hast einen Dummkopf schonen wollen,
Und zwölfe sind es, die dir grollen.

WELTLAUF

Hat man viel, so wird man bald
Noch viel mehr dazu bekommen.
Wer nur wenig hat, dem wird
Auch das Wenige genommen.

Wenn du aber gar nichts hast,
Ach, so lasse dich begraben—
Denn ein Recht zum Leben, Lump,
Haben nur, die etwas haben.

Never should I advocate
Thus to speak before the people,
Thus to speak about the preachers,
Or of any potentate.

My dear friend, I have my fears!
Very long arms have the princes,
Very long tongues have the preachers,
And the people have long ears.

GOOD ADVICE

You better give your model's name
To every hero of your fable,
For, if you don't, you will enable
A dozen gray old fools to claim:
"Those surely are my own long ears,
And that, moreover, is my fierce
And powerful terrific bray.
I am that ass," each one will say,
"Although he does not give my name,
My fatherland Germania
Will recognize me all the same.
I am that ass! Ee-aw, ee-aw!"

You tried to spare one ass's head
And you made enemies of twelve instead.

THE WAY OF THE WORLD

Those who have much will one day
Suddenly with more awaken;
But from him who has but little
Even that will soon be taken.

If you have not anything—
Well, you'd better dig your grave,
For, a right to live, you bum,
Have but those alone who have.

DER NEUE GLAUBE

Auf diesem Felsen bauen wir
Die Kirche von dem dritten,
Dem dritten neuen Testament;
Das Leid ist ausgelitten.

Vernichtet ist das Zweierlei,
Das uns so lang betöret;
Die dumme Leiberquälerei
Hat endlich aufgehöret.

Hörst du den Gott im finstern Meer?
Mit tausend Stimmen spricht er.
Und siehst du über unserm Haupt
Die tausend Gotteslichter?

Der heil'ge Gott der ist im Licht
Wie in den Finsternissen;
Und Gott ist alles, was da ist;
Er ist in unsern Küssen.

JETZT WOHIN?

Jetzt wohin? Der dumme Fuß
Will mich gern nach Deutschland tragen;
Doch es schüttelt klug das Haupt
Mein Verstand und scheint zu sagen:

Zwar beendigt ist der Krieg,
Doch die Kriegsgerichte blieben,
Und es heißt, du habest einst
Viel Erschießliches geschrieben.

Das ist wahr, unangenehm
Wär mir das Erschossenwerden;
Bin kein Held, es fehlen mir
Die pathetischen Gebärden.

THE NEW CREED

Upon this rock we shall erect
The church of the amended,
The third and true New Testament;
All suffering is ended.

The dualism is destroyed
From which our mind was ailing;
The stupid torment of the flesh
No longer is prevailing.

You hear God's voice from thousand lands,
From darkest sea resounding?
You see above in nightly sky
God's thousand lights abounding?

The holy God is in the light
As in the dark abysses;
And God is everything that is,
He, too, is in our kisses.

WHITHER NOW?

Whither now? My foot so foolish
Wants to go to Germany,
But my common sense, much wiser,
Shakes its head and seems to say:

To be sure, the war is ended,
But courts-martial still exist,
And as shootable offenses
Books of yours are on the list.

Yes, that's true, and most unpleasant,
I believe, is being shot;
Lacking highfalutin' gestures,
Real hero I am not.

Gern würd ich nach England gehn,
Wären dort nicht Kohlendämpfe
Und Engländer—schon ihr Duft
Gibt Erbrechen mir und Krämpfe.

Manchmal kommt mir in den Sinn,
Nach Amerika zu segeln,
Nach dem großen Freiheitstall,
Der bewohnt von Gleicheitsflegeln—

Doch es ängstigt mich ein Land,
Wo die Menschen Tabak käuen,
Wo sie ohne König kegeln,
Wo sie ohne Spucknapf speien.

Rußland, dieses schöne Reich,
Würde mir vielleicht behagen,
Doch im Winter könnte ich
Dort die Knute nicht vertragen.

Traurig schau ich in die Höh,
Wo viel tausend Sterne nicken—
Aber meinen eignen Stern
Kann ich nirgends dort erblicken.

Hat im güldnen Labyrinth
Sich vielleicht verirrt am Himmel,
Wie ich selber mich verirrt
In dem irdischen Getümmel.

Gladly would I go to England
Were it not for softcoal smoke,
And the English—just to smell them
Makes me vomit, cough and choke.

Sometimes west my mind will wander
Where America allures,
To the great cowbarn of freedom,
To the egalitarian boors.

But I am afraid of countries
Where they all tobacco chew,
Where they bowl without a kingpin
And have no spittoons to spew.

Russia, such a pleasant realm,
Might attract me, without doubt,
But I could not in their winter
Bear the feeling of a knout.

Sadly I look to the thousand
Twinkling stars that dot the sky—
But my own star I can nowhere
In their multitude espy.

In the labyrinth of golden
Stars perhaps it lost its way,
Just as in this earthly tumult
I myself have gone astray.

ERINNERUNG AUS
KRÄHWINKELS
SCHRECKENSTAGEN

Wir, Bürgermeister und Senat,
Wir haben folgendes Mandat
Stadtväterlichst an alle Klassen
Der treuen Bürgerschaft erlassen:

„Ausländer, Fremde, sind es meist,
Die unter uns gesät den Geist
Der Rebellion. Dergleichen Sünder,
Gottlob! sind selten Landeskinder.

„Auch Gottesleugner sind es meist;
Wer sich von seinem Gotte reißt,
Wird endlich auch abtrünnig werden
Von seinen irdischen Behörden.

„Der Obrigkeit gehorchen, ist
Die erste Pflicht für Jud' und Christ.
Es schließe jeder seine Bude,
Sobald es dunkelt, Christ und Jude.

„Wo ihrer drei beisammen stehn,
Da soll man auseinander gehn.
Des Nachts soll niemand auf den Gassen
Sich ohne Leuchte sehen lassen.

„Es liefre seine Waffen aus
Ein jeder in dem Gildenhaus;
Auch Munition von jeder Sorte
Wird deponiert am selben Orte.

„Wer auf der Straße räsoniert,
Wird unverzüglich füsiliert;
Das Räsonieren durch Gebärden
Soll gleichfalls hart bestrafet werden.

RECOLLECTION OF
CROWCORNER'S
DAYS OF TERROR

Mayor and city council, We
Issue the following decree
In city-father love to all
And every one within our wall:

"Foreigners, strangers from afar
With spirit of rebellion, mar
Our city life. Such kind of sin
Thank God! is rare among our kin.

"Atheists generally such are;
And who from God once strays so far
Will in disloyalty berate
His own good city magistrate.

"Obeisance to the law observe
Christian and Jew, and never swerve!
And every shop, Christian or Jew,
Shall close exactly at curfew!

"Where there are three together late,
They are enjoined to separate.
Nobody in the street at night
Shall wander 'round without a light.

"Weapons shall be by each and all
At once delivered at Guild Hall,
Which place will also take prompt charge
Of ammunition, small and large.

"Who on the streets will carp and peeve
Is shot at once without reprieve;
To carp and grumble with your hands
Will likewise be a grave offence.

„Vertrauet eurem Magistrat,
Der fromm und liebend schützt den Staat
Durch huldreich hochwohlweises Walten;
Euch ziemt es stets, das Maul zu halten."

DIE WANDERRATTEN

Es gibt zwei Sorten Ratten:
Die hungrigen und die satten.
Die satten bleiben vergnügt zu Haus,
Die hungrigen aber wandern aus.

Sie wandern viel tausend Meilen,
Ganz ohne Rasten und Weilen,
Gradaus in ihrem grimmigen Lauf,
Nicht Wind noch Wetter hält sie auf.

Sie klimmen wohl über die Höhen,
Sie schwimmen wohl durch die Seen;
Gar manche ersäuft oder bricht das Genick,
Die lebenden lassen die toten zurück.

Es haben diese Käuze
Gar fürchterliche Schnäuze;
Sie tragen die Köpfe geschoren egal,
Ganz radikal, ganz rattenkahl.

Die radikale Rotte
Weiß nichts von einem Gotte.
Sie lassen nicht taufen ihre Brut,
Die Weiber sind Gemeindegut.

Der sinnliche Rattenhaufen
Er will nur fressen und saufen,
Er denkt nicht, während er säuft und frißt,
Daß unsre Seele unsterblich ist.

"Confide in your kind magistrate,
Who lovingly protects the state,
Takes all your cares onto his lap;
Your duty is to shut your trap."

THE MIGRATORY RATS

There are two kinds of rat,
The hungry and the fat;
The fat ones happily stay at home,
But the hungry ones set out to roam.

They wander thousands of miles,
They have no domiciles;
Straight on they move in a furious run,
They cannot be stopped by rain or sun.

No mountains they cannot skim,
No lakes too broad for their swim!
Many get drowned or break their necks,
But those who survive pass over the wrecks.

These queer peculiar louts
Grow whiskers above their snouts;
As radical egalitarians they wear
In ratty fashion close-cropped their hair.

This fierce and radical squad
Knows no eternal God;
Unbaptized they leave their numerous broods,
They keep their women as common goods.

A sensuous mob, they think
Only of food and drink;
They ignore, since food is their only goal,
The immortality of the soul.

So eine wilde Ratze
Die fürchtet nicht Hölle, nicht Katze;
Sie hat kein Gut, sie hat kein Geld
Und wünscht aufs neue zu teilen die Welt.

Die Wanderraten, o wehe!
Sie sind schon in der Nähe.
Sie rücken heran, ich höre schon
Ihr Pfeifen, die Zahl ist Legion.

O wehe! wir sind verloren,
Sie sind schon vor den Toren!
Der Bürgermeister und Senat,
Sie schütteln die Köpfe, und keiner weiß Rat.

Die Bürgerschaft greift zu den Waffen,
Die Glocken läuten die Pfaffen.
Gefährdet ist das Palladium
Des sittlichen Staats, das Eigentum.

Nicht Glockengeläute, nicht Pfaffengebete,
Nicht hochwohlweise Senatsdekrete,
Auch nicht Kanonen, viel Hundertpfünder,
Sie helfen euch heute, ihr lieben Kinder!

Heut helfen euch nicht die Wortgespinste
Der abgelebten Redekünste.
Man fängt nicht Ratten mit Syllogismen,
Sie springen über die feinsten Sophismen.

Im hungrigen Magen Eingang finden
Nur Suppenlogik mit Knödelgründen,
Nur Argumente von Rinderbraten,
Begleitet mit Göttinger Wurstzitaten.

Ein schweigender Stockfisch, in Butter gesotten,
Behaget den radikalen Rotten
Viel besser als ein Mirabeau
Und alle Redner seit Cicero.

For such a brutal rat
Fears neither hell nor cat;
No goods, nor money they ever acquire,
To redivide the world they desire.

Approaching I see the foe
Of wandering rats, oh woe!
They come, already they are at our heels,
Their number is legion, I hear their squeals.

Oh woe! now we are lost!
At our portal their awful host!
The council and mayor shake their heads,
They despair of warding off those reds.

The burghers take up arms,
The blackfrocks ring the alarms;
The paladium of public morality,
Property, is in jeopardy.

No ringing of bells, no priestly pleas,
No wise and august council decrees,
Not even cannons of widest gage
Will help you, my children, against their rage.

No help you will find in verbal trick
Of worn political rhetoric;
You can't catch rats with syllogisms,
They nimbly jump your finest sophisms.

Soup-logic only and reason-dumplings
Will silence their hungry stomach rumblings,
Or arguments of soup donations
Together with Göttingen sausage quotations.

A silent codfish in butter fat
Will satisfy such a radical rat
Much better than any Mirabeau
And all the orations since Cicero.

DIE SCHLESISCHEN WEBER

Im düstern Auge keine Träne,
Sie sitzen am Webstuhl und fletschen die Zähne:
„Deutschland, wir weben dein Leichentuch,
Wir weben hinein den dreifachen Fluch—
    Wir weben, wir weben!

„Ein Fluch dem Gotte, zu dem wir gebeten
In Winterskälte und Hungersnöten;
Wir haben vergebens gehofft und geharrt,
Er hat uns geäfft und gefoppt und genarrt—
    Wir weben, wir weben!

„Ein Fluch dem König, dem König der Reichen,
Den unser Elend nicht konnte erweichen,
Der den letzten Groschen von uns erpreßt,
Und uns wie Hunde erschießen läßt—
    Wir weben, wir weben!

„Ein Fluch dem falschen Vaterlande,
Wo nur gedeihen Schmach und Schande,
Wo jede Blume früh geknickt,
Wo Fäulnis und Moder den Wurm erquickt—
    Wir weben, wir weben!

„Das Schiffchen fliegt, der Webstuhl kracht,
Wir weben emsig bei Tag und Nacht—
Altdeutschland, wir weben dein Leichentuch,
Wir weben hinein den dreifachen Fluch,
    Wir weben, wir weben!"

THE SILESIAN WEAVERS

No tears they shed from eyes of doom,
Gnashing their teeth they sit at the loom:
"A shroud for Germany we weave
With a triple curse—and no reprieve!
    We are weaving, we are weaving!

"A curse on the God to whom we prayed,
Who left us hungry, cold and dismayed;
We trusted and waited and hoped in vain,
He duped and fooled us again and again—
    We are weaving, we are weaving!

"A curse on the King of the rich, whose ear
Was deaf to our grief and blind to our tear,
Who took the last penny out of our purse
And had us shot like mangy curs.
    We are weaving, we are weaving!

"A curse on the fatherland, where apace
Grow the wealth of the rich, and our shame and disgrace
Where every bud is felled by a blight,
Where rot and decay feed the parasite—
We are weaving, we are weaving.

"The loom groans with the shuttle's flight,
We are busy weaving by day and by night—
A shroud for Old Germany we weave
With a triple curse—and no reprieve!
    We are weaving, we are weaving!"

VI

LAMENTATIONS
LAMENTATIONEN

IN DER FREMDE

Ich hatte einst ein schönes Vaterland.
Der Eichenbaum
Wuchs dort so hoch, die Veilchen nickten sanft.
Es war ein Traum.

Das küßte mich auf deutsch und sprach auf deutsch
(Man glaubt es kaum
Wie gut es klang) das Wort: „Ich liebe dich!"
Es war ein Traum.

AN DIE SCHWESTER

Mein Kind, wir waren Kinder,
Zwei Kinder klein und froh;
Wir krochen ins Hühnerhäuschen,
Versteckten uns unter das Stroh.

Wir krähten wie die Hähne,
Und kamen Leute vorbei—
Kikeriki! sie glaubten,
Es wäre Hahnengeschrei.

Die Kisten auf unserem Hofe,
Die tapezierten wir aus,
Und wohnten drin beisammen
Und machten ein vornehmes Haus.

Des Nachbars alte Katze
Kam öfters zum Besuch;
Wir machten ihr Bückling und Knickse
Und Komplimente genug.

Wir haben nach ihrem Befinden
Besorglich und freundlich gefragt,
Wir haben seitdem dasselbe
Mancher alten Katze gesagt.

IN FOREIGN LANDS

One time I had a lovely fatherland.
The oak grew high
And under it would gentle violets stand.
A dream—gone by.

The land that kissed me, spoke to me in German—
Who could tell why
So sweet did sound the words "I love you"—
A dream—gone by.

TO HIS SISTER

My child, when we were children,
Two children small and gay,
We crept into the henhouse
And hid beneath the hay.

We crowed just like a rooster,
If anyone went by—
Cockadoodledoo, they really
Believed it a rooster's cry.

The boxes in our courtyard
We papered after a while,
And there we lived together
And put on airs and style.

The cat of our nearest neighbor
Came often to our door;
We made her bows and curtsies
And compliments galore.

We asked how she was feeling
In an anxious and friendly chat;
We have often said the same since
To many an old cat.

Wir saßen auch oft und sprachen
Vernünftig wie alte Leut,
Und klagten, wie alles besser
Gewesen zu unserer Zeit;

Wie Lieb und Treu und Glauben
Verschwunden aus der Welt,
Und wie so teuer der Kaffee,
Und wie so rar das Geld!—

Vorbei sind die Kinderspiele,
Und alles rollt vorbei—
Das Geld und die Welt und die Zeiten
Und Glauben und Lieb und Treu.

ANNO 1839

O Deutschland, meine ferne Liebe,
Gedenk ich deiner, wein ich fast!
Das muntre Frankreich scheint mir trübe,
Das leichte Volk wird mir zur Last.

Nur der Verstand, so kalt und trocken,
Herrscht in dem witzigen Paris—
O, Narrheitsglöcklein, Glaubensglocken,
Wie klingelt ihr daheim so süß!

Höfliche Männer! Doch verdrossen
Geb ich den art'gen Gruß zurück.—
Die Grobheit, die ich einst genossen
Im Vaterland, das war mein Glück!

Lächelnde Weiber! Plappern immer,
Wie Mühlenräder stets bewegt!
Da lob ich Deutschlands Frauenzimmer,
Das schweigend sich zu Bette legt.

And often we talked like grown-ups
Full of sense with many a sigh,
Complaining how all was better
In the good old days gone by;

How loyalty, love and religion
No longer were as of old,
And how so expensive the coffee,
And how so rare the gold!—

Gone is our childish playing,
And everything rolls like a ball—
Time and the world and money,
Faith, loyalty, love and all.

ANNO 1839

Oh Germany, so dear and distant,
Thinking of you I almost cry!
To cheerful France I seem resistant
And to her folk, so light and spry.

In Paris, reason, cold, unfeeling,
Reigns, full of wit and indiscreet—
Ah, foolscaptinkles, churchbells' pealing
For faithfuls sound at home so sweet.

Such courteous men! Somewhat ungracious
I answer their polite address.—
Our German rudeness, though vexatious,
It added to my happiness.

And smiling women, so loquacious,
Like millwheels always turning 'round!
Our German women, less vivacious,
Just go to bed without a sound.

Und alles dreht sich hier im Kreise,
Mit Ungestüm, wie'n toller Traum!
Bei uns bleibt alles hübsch im Gleise,
Wie angenagelt, rührt sich kaum.

Mir ist, als hört ich fern erklingen
Nachtwächterhörner, sanft und traut;
Nachtwächterlieder hör ich singen,
Dazwischen Nachtigallenlaut.

Dem Dichter war so wohl daheime,
In Schildas teurem Eichenhain!
Dort wob ich meine zarten Reime
Aus Veilchenduft und Mondenschein.

NACHTGEDANKEN

Denk ich an Deutschland in der Nacht,
Dann bin ich um den Schlaf gebracht,
Ich kann nicht mehr die Augen schließen,
Und meine heißen Tränen fließen.

Die Jahre kommen und vergehn!
Seit ich die Mutter nicht gesehn,
Zwölf Jahre sind schon hingegangen;
Es wächst mein Sehnen und Verlangen.

Mein Sehnen und Verlangen wächst.
Die alte Frau hat mich behext,
Ich denke immer an die alte,
Die alte Frau, die Gott erhalte!

Die alte Frau hat mich so lieb,
Und in den Briefen, die sie schrieb,
Seh ich, wie ihre Hand gezittert,
Wie tief das Mutterherz erschüttert.

162

And everything here keeps on moving
In wild confusion, like a dream!
At home things stay in their old grooving,
Nailed down forever, it would seem.

Methinks I hear the far saluting
Of nightwatchman's familiar hail;
Nightwatchman's song and gentle tooting
And in between the nightingale.

How much at home in those old cities
The poet felt, 'twixt oaken groves,
Where I my tender little ditties
Of violet scent and moonlight wove.

NIGHT THOUGHTS

Thinking of Germany at night
Just puts all thought of sleep to flight;
No longer I can close an eye,
Tears gather and I start to cry.

So many years have come and passed
Since I saw my old mother last,
Twelve years I have seen come and go;
My yearning and my longing grow.

My longing's grown since our farewell.
Perhaps she cast on me a spell,
The good old woman; I can't sleep
And think of her—whom God may keep.

From all her letters I must see
How deep the love she feels for me,
The tremblings of her hand betray
More than her trembling heart would say.

Die Mutter liegt mir stets im Sinn.
Zwölf lange Jahre flossen hin,
Zwölf lange Jahre sind verflossen,
Seit ich sie nicht ans Herz geschlossen.

Deutschland hat ewigen Bestand,
Es ist ein kerngesundes Land;
Mit seinen Eichen, seinen Linden
Werd ich es immer wiederfinden.

Nach Deutschland lechzt ich nicht so sehr,
Wenn nicht die Mutter dorten wär;
Das Vaterland wird nie verderben,
Jedoch die alte Frau kann sterben.

Seit ich das Land verlassen hab,
So viele sanken dort ins Grab,
Die ich geliebt—wenn ich sie zähle,
So will verbluten meine Seele.

Und zählen muß ich—Mit der Zahl
Schwillt immer höher meine Qual,
Mir ist, als wälzten sich die Leichen
Auf meine Brust—Gottlob! sie weichen!

Gottlob! durch meine Fenster bricht
Französisch heitres Tageslicht;
Es kommt mein Weib, schön wie der Morgen,
Und lächelt fort die deutschen Sorgen.

GESUCH

Mich locken nicht die Himmelsauen
Im Paradies, im sel'gen Land;
Dort find ich keine schönre Frauen,
Als ich bereits auf Erden fand.

The mother's always in my mind,
Already twelve years lie behind,
Twelve long years since I did depart
And clasped the mother to my heart.

Germany will for evermore
Endure; she's healthy to the core;
Returning I shall always find
Her oaks and lindens left behind.

My longing for her I could bear
But for the good old woman there;
There always will be Germany,
But the old mother may pass away.

And since I left the Fatherland,
The grave has claimed so many a friend
Whom I have loved—I count the toll
And fear to death will bleed my soul.

And count I must, and as I count
My torment and their numbers mount;
I feel how their dead bodies heave
Upon my breast—thank God, they leave!

Thank God—for a French morning light
Breaks through my window gay and bright;
My wife, resplendent as the day
Smiles all my German cares away.

PETITION

Celestial fields have little lure
For me; those of this earth suffice;
Handsomer women, I am sure,
I can not find in paradise.

Kein Engel mit den feinsten Schwingen
Könnt mir ersetzen dort mein Weib;
Auf Wolken sitzend Psalmen singen,
Wär auch nicht just mein Zeitvertreib.

O Herr! ich glaub, es wär das Beste
Du ließest mich in dieser Welt;
Heil nur zuvor mein Leibgebreste,
Und sorge auch für etwas Geld.

Ich weiß, es ist voll Sünd und Laster
Die Welt; jedoch ich bin einmal
Gewöhnt, auf diesem Erdpechpflaster
Zu schlendern durch das Jammertal.

Genieren wird das Weltgetreibe
Mich nie, denn selten geh ich aus;
Im Schlafrock und Pantoffeln bleibe
Ich gern bei meiner Frau zu Haus.

Laß mich bei ihr! Hör ich sie schwätzen,
Trinkt meine Seele die Musik
Der holden Stimme mit Ergötzen.
So treu und ehrlich ist ihr Blick!

Gesundheit nur und Geldzulage
Verlang ich, Herr! O laß mich froh
Hinleben noch viel schöne Tage
Bei meiner Frau im statu quo!

DER ABGEKÜHLTE

Und ist man tot, so muß man lang
Im Grabe liegen; ich bin bang,
Ja, ich bin bang, das Auferstehen
Wird nicht so schnell von statten gehen.

No angel of the finest wing
Could up above replace my wife;
To sit on clouds and psalms to sing
Would not be my ideal life.

I think, oh Lord, the best would be
To leave me on this earth below;
But first restore my health to me,
And then provide a little dough.

I know the world is full of sin;
But I got used—in all these years—
To sauntering amidst the din
On asphalt through this vale of tears.

Nor does the tumult and the fray
Annoy me; I'm not one to roam;
In slippers and in bathrobe stay
Peacefully with my wife at home.

Leave me with her! I love to hear
Her charming voice; her chat, so spry,
Is always music to my ear;
And true and honest is her eye.

Health only and a little raise
I ask, my Lord! Oh let me so
Live on for many a happy year
With my good wife in statu quo!

TEMPERATE LOVE

We must stay buried once we're dead
For quite a while, I am afraid,
Yes, I'm afraid time won't go fast
Till resurrection comes at last.

Noch einmal, eh mein Lebenslicht
Erlöschet, eh mein Herze bricht—
Noch einmal möcht ich vor dem Sterben
Um Frauenhuld beseligt werben.

Und eine Blonde müßt es sein,
Mit Augen sanft wie Mondenschein—
Denn schlecht bekommen mir am Ende
Die wild brünetten Sonnenbrände.

Das junge Volk voll Lebenskraft
Will den Tumult der Leidenschaft,
Das ist ein Rasen, Schwören, Poltern
Und wechselseit'ges Seelenfoltern!

Unjung und nicht mehr ganz gesund,
Wie ich es bin zu dieser Stund,
Möcht ich noch einmal lieben, schwärmen
Und glücklich sein—doch ohne Lärmen.

GEDÄCHTNISFEIER

Keine Messe wird man singen,
Keinen Kadosch wird man sagen,
Nichts gesagt und nichts gesungen
Wird an meinen Sterbetagen.

Doch vielleicht an solchem Tage,
Wenn das Wetter schön und milde,
Geht spazieren auf Montmartre
Mit Paulinen Frau Mathilde.

Mit dem Kranz von Immortellen
Kommt sie, mir das Grab zu schmücken,
Und sie seufzet: Pauvre homme!
Feuchte Wehmut in den Blicken.

Just once, I wish, before my light
Goes out and I give up the fight,
I wish I could before I die
Once more for woman's favor vie.

And blond must be that lady mine
With eyes like gentle Luna's shine—
For poorly I can now withstand
A stormy brunette firebrand.

The young folk, full of vital urge,
Delight in passion's violent surge;
That is a raving and insane
Mutual torturing and pain.

As, at this hour, I am unyoung
And not quite healthy, I do long
Once more to feel a youth's devotion,
To love, adore—but sans commotion.

MEMORIAL DAY

Not a mass will there be chanted,
Not a Kaddish will be said,
Nothing will be sung nor spoken
In memoriam when I'm dead.

But perhaps on such a morning
When the weather's nice and warm
Will my wife go to Montmartre,
She and Pauline arm in arm.

With the wreath of everlastings
For my grave she then may come
And, moist sadness in her glances,
She will sigh: mon pauvre homme.

Leider wohn ich viel zu hoch,
Und ich habe meiner Süßen
Keinen Stuhl hier anzubieten;
Ach! sie schwankt mit müden Füßen.

Süßes, dickes Kind, du darfst
Nicht zu Fuß nach Hause gehen;
An dem Barrière-Gitter
Siehst du die Fiaker stehen.

LAZARUS

1

Laß die heil'gen Parabolen,
Laß die frommen Hypothesen—
Suche die verdammten Fragen
Ohne Umschweif uns zu lösen.

Warum schleppt sich blutend, elend,
Unter Kreuzlast der Gerechte,
Während glücklich als ein Sieger
Trabt auf hohem Roß der Schlechte?

Woran liegt die Schuld? Ist etwa
Unser Herr nicht ganz allmächtig?
Oder treibt er selbst den Unfug?
Ach, das wäre niederträchtig.

Also fragen wir beständig,
Bis man uns mit einer Handvoll
Erde endlich stopft die Mäuler—
Aber ist das eine Antwort?

2

Wie langsam kriechet sie dahin,
Die Zeit, die schauderhafte Schnecke!
Ich aber, ganz bewegungslos
Blieb ich hier auf demselben Flecke.

Too bad I live up so high,
Cannot offer to my sweet
Any chair for her to rest on,
Oh, she sways on weary feet.

Darling chubby, do not walk
Home, for you are far too tired;
At the city gate there always
Are some cabs that can be hired.

LAZARUS

1

Drop those parables of Scripture,
Drop the hypothetic phrases!
Seek to solve without evasion
Those damn problems that amaze us.

Why, triumphant as a victor,
Rides his steed the viler, bolder,
While the just one, stumbling, panting,
Bears his cross on bleeding shoulder?

Whose the blame? Is not almighty,
As we think, God in His heaven?
Does He have His sport with mortals?
Ah—that would be downright craven.

Thus we ask in vain until they
Stuff our mouths just with a handful
Of the earth from which we're taken.
But, pray tell, is that an answer?

2

How slowly Time, the loathsome snail,
Keeps crawling in its slimy trace!
But I, meanwhile, quite motionless,
Must bide here in this selfsame place.

In meine dunkle Zelle dringt
Kein Sonnenstrahl, kein Hoffnungsschimmer;
Ich weiß, nur mit der Kirchhofsgruft
Vertausch ich dies fatale Zimmer.

Vielleicht bin ich gestorben längst;
Es sind vielleicht nur Spukgestalten
Die Phantasieen, die des Nachts
Im Hirn den bunten Umzug halten.

Es mögen wohl Gespenster sein
Altheidnisch göttlichen Gelichters;
Sie wählen gern zum Tummelplatz
Den Schädel eines toten Dichters.—

Die schaurig süßen Orgia
Das nächtlich tolle Geistertreiben,
Sucht des Poeten Leichenhand
Manchmal am Morgen aufzuschreiben.

3

Vom Schöppenstuhle der Vernunft
Bist du vollständig freigesprochen;
Das Urteil sagt: die Kleine hat
Durch Tun und Reden nichts verbrochen.

Ja, stumm und tatlos standest du,
Als mich verzehrten tolle Flammen—
Du schürtest nicht, du sprachst kein Wort,
Und doch muß dich mein Herz verdammen.

In meinen Träumen jede Nacht
Klagt eine Stimme, die bezichtet
Des bösen Willens dich, und sagt,
Du habest mich zugrund gerichtet.

No ray of sun, no gleam of hope
Will fall into my darkened room;
I know I'll trade this baneful cell
For nothing but the churchyard tomb.

Perhaps I have died long ago;
And only spooks may be those vain
Phantasms, pageants, which at night
In wild array storm through my brain.

Or afterwalkers they could be,
Old pagan gods, an ilk of Hell;
They love to choose their rousting place
In a dead poet's empty skull.—

Then sometimes would seek to record
At dawn the poet's mummied hand
Those awesome lurid orgia
Of specters in nocturnal band.

3

Before the judgement seat of reason
You have been quite completely freed;
The verdict says: the little lady
Has sinned by neither word nor deed.

Yes, you stood mute and you did nothing
While by wild flames I was consumed—
You did not fan them, you said nothing,
Yet, by my heart's voice you are doomed.

And in my dreams at every nightfall
A voice indicts you of bad will,
And this accuser says you're guilty
That I am ruined, down and ill.

Sie bringt Beweis und Zeugnis bei,
Sie schleppt ein Bündel von Urkunden;
Jedoch am Morgen, mit dem Traum,
Ist auch die Klägerin verschwunden.

Sie hat in meines Herzens Grund
Mit ihren Akten sich geflüchtet—
Nur eins bleibt im Gedächtnis mir,
Das ist: ich bin zugrund gerichtet.

4

Ein Wetterstrahl, beleuchtend plötzlich
Des Abgrunds Nacht, war mir dein Brief;
Er zeigte blendend hell, wie tief
Mein Unglück ist, wie tief entsetzlich.

Selbst dich ergreift ein Mitgefühl!
Dich, die in meines Lebens Wildnis
So schweigsam standest, wie ein Bildnis,
Das marmorschön und marmorkühl.

O Gott, wie muß ich elend sein!
Denn sie sogar beginnt zu sprechen,
Aus ihrem Auge Tränen brechen,
Der Stein sogar erbarmt sich mein!

Erschüttert hat mich, was ich sah!
Auch du erbarm dich mein und spende
Die Ruhe mir, o Gott, und ende
Die schreckliche Tragödia.

5

Stunden, Tage, Ewigkeiten
Sind es, die wie Schnecken gleiten;
Diese grauen Riesenschnecken
Ihre Hörner weit ausrecken.

174

Furnishing proof and testimony,
He drags a sheaf of documents;
But with the dream at every daybreak
The plaintiff always has gone hence.

By day he hides with all his papers
Deep in my heart, and is there still—
And only one thing I remember,
That is: I'm ruined, down and ill.

4

A thunderbolt your letter is,
Revealing in a blinding light
How deep, how horrible the night
Of my misfortune's deep abyss.

Your heart I even see unfold!
In my life's chaos you alone
Stood like an image, hewn in stone,
Mute marble, beautiful and cold.

Oh God, how wretched must I be!
For even she begins to speak,
And even her eyes start to weep,
The stone is moved to pity me.

Unstrung I am by what I saw!
Have pity also, God, and send
Your peace to me, your rest, and end
The terrible tragedia.

5

Hours and days—eternal biding,
Slowly, slowly, snaillike gliding,
And these gray gigantic snails
Stretch their horns like groping flails.

Manchmal in der öden Leere,
Manchmal in dem Nebelmeere
Strahlt ein Licht, das süß und golden,
Wie die Augen meiner Holden.

Doch im selben Nu zerstäubet
Diese Wonne, und mir bleibet
Das Bewußtsein nur, das schwere,
Meiner schrecklichen Misere.

6

Wie schön er ist, so qualvoll auch
Mit seinen Feuerbränden,
Ist dieses Lebens Fiebertraum—
Laß bald, o Gott, ihn enden.

Erschließe mir dein Schattenland,
Ich will die Lippe dort nässen
Mit jener Flut, die kühlend schenkt
Ein ewiges Vergessen.

Vergessen wird alles—die Liebe allein
Vergißt man nicht im Tode!
Das Märchen vom Lethestrand ersann
Ein griechisch liebloser Rhapsode.

MORPHINE

Groß ist die Ähnlichkeit der beiden schönen
Jünglingsgestalten, ob der eine gleich
Viel blässer als der andre, auch viel strenger,
Fast möcht ich sagen: viel vornehmer aussieht
Als jener andre, welcher mich vertraulich
In seine Arme schloß—Wie lieblich sanft
War dann sein Lächeln, und sein Blick wie selig!
Dann mocht es wohl geschehn, daß seines Hauptes
Mohnblumenkranz auch meine Stirn berührte

Sometimes in this desolation,
Sometimes in this obfuscation
Shines a light, so sweet and bright
Like my Love's, the golden eyed.

But to dust blows in a second
All that bliss again that beckoned,
And I'm conscious of my bare
Crushing terrible misère.

6

However beautiful this life,
A fever dream, heartrending
With all its firebrands it is;
Oh God, see to its ending.

Unlock your shadowland to me,
Grant me the fount that, wetting
My lips with yonder cooling flow,
Bestows eternal forgetting.

Forgotten is all—but love alone
Remains when life is ended!
By a loveless Grecian rhapsodist
Was the legend of Lethe invented.

MORPHINE

Great is the likeness of those beauteous two,
The youthful brothers, though the one appears
Much paler than the other, also much
More stern, yes, I might almost say much more
Aristocratic than that one who clasped me
Tenderly in his arm—How sweetly gentle
Was then his smile, his glance so full of bliss!
Thus it would happen that his wreath of poppies,
His head encircling, grazed my forehead also

Und seltsam duftend allen Schmerz verscheuchte
Aus meiner Seel—Doch solche Linderung,
Sie dauert kurze Zeit; genesen gänzlich
Kann ich nur dann, wenn seine Fackel senkt
Der andre Bruder, der so ernst und bleich.—
Gut ist der Schlaf, der Tot ist besser—freilich
Das beste wäre, nie geboren sein.

AN DIE ENGEL

Das ist der böse Thanatos,
Er kommt auf einem fahlen Roß;
Ich hör den Hufschlag, hör den Trab,
Der dunkle Reiter holt mich ab—
Er reißt mich fort, Mathilden soll ich lassen,
O, den Gedanken kann mein Herz nicht fassen!

Sie war mir Weib und Kind zugleich,
Und geh ich in das Schattenreich,
Wird Wittwe sie und Waise sein!
Ich laß in dieser Welt allein
Das Weib, das Kind, das, trauend meinem Mute,
Sorglos und treu an meinem Herzen ruhte.

Ihr Engel in den Himmelshöhn,
Vernehmt mein Schluchzen und mein Flehn;
Beschützt, wenn ich im öden Grab,
Das Weib, das ich geliebet hab;
Seid Schild und Vögte eurem Ebenbilde,
Beschützt, beschirmt mein armes Kind, Mathilde.

Bei allen Tränen, die ihr je
Geweint um unser Menschenweh,
Beim Wort, das nur der Priester kennt
Und niemals ohne Schauder nennt,
Bei eurer eignen Schönheit, Huld und Milde,
Beschwör ich euch, ihr Engel, schützt Mathilde.

And with strange fragrance banished all the pain
Out of my soul—Yet such a kind reprieve
It lasts but a short while, because completely
Restored can I be only when his brother,
The stern and pallid one, inverts his torch.—
Oh, sleep is good, death better—to be sure,
The best of all were not to have been born.

TO THE ANGELS

That is the wicked Thanatos,
He rides upon a fallow horse;
I hear its hoofbeat, hear its gait,
The cruel horseman lies in wait—
He'll tear me hence, Mathilde I must leave,
Oh, how that thought does my poor heart bereave.

To me she was both child and wife,
And if I pass to yonder life,
Widow and orphan she will be,
Forsaken in this world by me,
My wife, my child, who in my courage trusted,
Carefree and loyal on my bosom rested.

You angels far above the skies,
Oh hear my sobbing and my cries,
Protect, when I am laid to rest
My angel wife, the loved and bless'd;
Be shield and warden to your own reflection:
My child Mathilde, grant her your protection.

By all the tears wept from your eyes
For human woes and human sighs
And by the name the priest alone
May speak and shudderingly intone,
By your own beauty, clemency, perfection
I pray: you angels, grant her your protection.

GESTÄNDNIS

Es kommt der Tod—jetzt will ich sagen,
Was zu verschweigen ewiglich
Mein Stolz gebot: für dich, für dich,
Es hat mein Herz für dich geschlagen

Der Sarg ist fertig, sie versenken
Mich in die Gruft. Da hab ich Ruh.
Doch du, doch du, Maria, du,
Wirst weinen oft und mein gedenken.

Du ringst sogar die schönen Hände—
O tröste dich—Das ist das Los,
Das Menschenlos:—was gut und groß
Und schön, das nimmt ein schlechtes Ende.

SIE ERLISCHT

Der Vorhang fällt, das Stück ist aus,
Und Herrn und Damen gehn nach Haus.
Ob ihnen auch das Stück gefallen?
Ich glaub, ich hörte Beifall schallen.
Ein hochverehrtes Publikum
Beklatschte dankbar seinen Dichter.
Jetzt aber ist das Haus so stumm,
Und sind verschwunden Lust und Lichter.

Doch horch! ein schollernd schnöder Klang
Ertönt unfern der öden Bühne;—
Vielleicht daß eine Saite sprang
An einer alten Violine.
Verdrießlich rascheln im Parterr
Etwelche Ratten hin und her,
Und alles riecht nach ranz'gem Öle.
Die letzte Lampe ächzt und zischt
Verzweiflungsvoll und sie erlischt.
Das arme Licht war meine Seele.

AVOWAL

Death comes—and now I shall avow
What pride so long bid me conceal:
My love for you I must reveal,
I've always loved you, love you now.

The coffin's ready—presently
They sink me in the grave. I do
Have peace; but you, Maria, you
Will weep and will remember me.

You'll even wring your dainty hands—
Oh, be consoled—That is the fate
The human fate: what's good and great
And beautiful, in misery ends.

THE LIGHT GOES OUT

The curtain falls, the play is done.
Ladies and gentlemen are gone.
Did they believe the play worth lauding?
I think I noticed some applauding.
An estimable audience
Paid to its poet due tribute,
But now the house is dark and mute
And lights and gayety went hence.

Yet hark! a mean and rumbling clang
Resounds from the deserted stage;—
Perhaps a string burst with a twang
On some old fiddle, weak with age.
Some rats rustle in peevish fit
Hither and thither in the pit
And rancid oil smell fills the whole.
The last lamp flickers low and sighs
Full of despair, gives up and dies.
The piteous light was my own soul.

181

WO?

Wo wird einst des Wandermüden
Letzte Ruhestätte sein?
Unter Palmen in dem Süden?
Unter Linden an dem Rhein?

Werd ich wo in einer Wüste
Eingescharrt von fremder Hand?
Oder ruh ich an der Küste
Eines Meeres in dem Sand?

Immerhin! Mich wird umgeben
Gotteshimmel, dort wie hier,
Und als Totenlampen schweben
Nachts die Sterne über mir.

WHERE?

Where when I am wander-wearied
Is my resting place to be?
Shall I under palms be buried?
Under Rhenish linden tree?

Or will somewhere in the desert
Heel me in a stranger's hand?
Shall I rest by some strange hazard
On a seacoast in the sand?

Never mind! I'll be surrounded
By God's heaven where'er it be,
And, as candles, in the unbounded
Skies the stars are over me.

CHRONOLOGY
OF HEINE'S LIFE AND LETTERS

DÜSSELDORF   1797–1815
Born December 13
Private schools, lyceum,
commercial school   1804–14
FRANKFURT   1815
Apprenticeship in banking   Begins to write poetry
and grocery firms
HAMBURG   1816–19
In his uncle's banking firm,   First poems published in
then commission merchant;   *Hamburg's Wächter;* transla-
in love with his cousin   tions from Byron's *Childe*
Amalie   *Harold* and *Manfred*
BONN   1819–20
University, germanistic   Sonnets, essay: *Die Roman-*
and historical studies;   *tik*
Schlegel's influence
Political reaction; Carlsbad
decrees
GÖTTINGEN   1820–22
University, continuation of
studies and study of law
BERLIN   1821–23
University, same studies   *Gedichte* 1821, containing
and philosophy under   first lyrics and ballads (Bel-
Hegel; Association for Ju-   sazar, Grenadiere); journal-
daic Culture; trip to Po-   1822   ism: *Briefe aus Berlin*
land; visit to Hamburg:
in love with his cousin
Therese; at sea shore in
summer   1823   *Tragödien nebst einem lyri-*
schen Intermezzo, containing
Almansor, William Ratcliff,
poems written since 1821

GÖTTINGEN   1824–25
University, study of law;
hike through Harz Moun-
tains (Sept); baptism
(June) and doctor's de-
gree (July); plans of ha-   1825
bilitation or law practice
North Sea Shore

HAMBURG (Nov.-July)　　1825–26
Sea shore in summer　　　1826　　　*Reisebilder I,* 1826, containing Harz Journey, Songs of Homecoming, North Sea Odes I

LÜNEBURG (Sept.-Jan.)　　1826–27　　*Reisebilder II,* 1827, containing North Sea Odes II, The North Sea III (prose), Book Le Grand, Letters from Berlin
Hamburg (-April), London and sea shore in summer (-Sept.), then Hamburg and Lüneburg and to
Buch der Lieder, 1827, containing all poems written so far

MÜNCHEN　　　　　　　1827–28
Editor of the New General Political Annals; hopes for a professorship; journey to Genoa, Lucca, Florence;　1828
death of his father (Dec.), return to Hamburg

BERLIN　　　　　　　　1829
Helgoland (Aug.-Sept.)

HAMBURG (Oct.-April)　　1829–31　　*Reisebilder III,* 1830, containing the Italian Journey, The Baths of Lucca
Helgoland (July-Aug. 1830)
Juli revolution in Paris

In spring over Hannover, Frankfurt, Heidelberg, Straßburg to Paris
Nachträge zu den Reisebildern, 1831, republished 1834 as *Reisebilder IV,* containing The City of Lucca, English Fragments, some poems of the later Neue Gedichte

From now on his permanent abode is Paris (1831–1856) where he remains except for a few journeys and his habitual summer vacations in sea resorts (Dieppe, Boulogne, Le Havre, Granville, Trouville), in the Pyrenees (Cauterets, Barèges) or in his last years in Montmorency near Paris.

Cholera in Paris　　　　1832

1833　　　*Französische Zustände,* 1833, containing reports on politics, etc., in France, written for the Augsburger Allgemeine Zeitung from Dec. 1831–Sept. 1832
Etat actuel de la littérature en Allgemagne in the journal L'Europe littéraire, 1833, in book form: *Zur Geschichte der neueren schönen Litteraatur in Deutschland,* 1833

Acquaintance with Eugénie Mirat, his "Mathilde" (Oct.)	1834	De l'Allemagne depuis Luther, in the Revue des Deux Mondes, 1834 Der Salon I, 1834, containing reviews of Paris art exhibitions, the satire Schnabelewopski and poems written since Buch der Lieder
Interest in Saint-Simonism		
Proscription of the writings of Young Germany by the German Diet and persecution of liberals	1835	Der Salon II, 1835, containing essay Zur Geschichte der Religion und Philosophie in Deutschland and poems
Quarrels with Mathilde and protracted stay Heine's at the manor of the Princess Belgiojoso		
French State Pension (until 1848)	1836	Die Romantische Schule, 1836, i.e. enlarged version of Zur Geschichte, etc.
Trip to Aix, Avingnon, Lyon to recover from jaundice		
Eye trouble	1837	Der Salon III, 1837, containing Preface (attacks on Menzel, Suabian poets), Florentine Nights, essay on legends of sprites
Visit of Uncle Salomon, who continues pension; Pfitzer attacks Heine	1838	Shakespeares Mädchen und Frauen, 1838, Schwabenspiegel in Jahrbuch der Literatur
	1840	Der Salon IV, 1840, containing poems, fragments of Rabbi von Bacharach, Letters on the French theater Ludwig Börne, eine Denkschrift, 1840
Ptosis of the eye; marriage with Mathilde; duell with Straus	1841	
Journey to Hamburg (Nov.-Dec.)	1843	Parts of Atta Troll in Zeitschrift für die elegante Welt (see below)
Journey to Hamburg (July-Oct.)	1844	Neue Gedichte, 1844, containing poems since Buch der Lieder and Deutschland, ein Wintermärchen, a satirical travelogue in verse
Salomon dies in December Inheritance quarrel		
First stroke, partial paralysis and beginning of "matress tumb"	1845	

Testament made; continuance of pension promised by Karl	1846
Visit of Karl	1847

Atta Troll, ein Sommernachtstraum 1847, humorous and satiric epic

February revolution in Paris	1848
Heine's last walk	
Slight temporary improvement	1849
	1851

Romanzero, 1851, containing ballads, "Lamentations," Hebraic Melodies
Der Doktor Faust, a ballet

Visit of his cousin Therese	1853
Visit of his sister Charlotte and his brother Gustav	1854

Vermischte Schriften, 1854, 3 vols. containing Poems 1853 and 1854, Confessions, The Gods in Exile, The Goddess Diana, Ludwig Marcus *Lutezia,* i.e., essays on life in Paris, originally written for Allgemeine Zeitung 1840–43

"Heine's last love," die "Mouche"	1855
Death, February 17	1856

Heine's "last poems and meditations" were published posthumously in 1869 by Adolf Strothmann as *Letzte Gedichte und Gedanken* and in 1884 by Eduard Engel *Heinrich Heines Memoiren.* There are so far two complete critical editions of Heine's works: *Heinrich Heines Sämtliche Werke,* herausgegeben von Professor Dr. Ernst Elster, Bibliographisches Institut, Leipzig und Wien, 1887–1890 (in seven volumes, four of which in a somewhat different arrangement were re-issued in a revised edition in 1924 ff.); and *Heinrich Heines Sämtliche Werke in Zehn Bänden,* herausgegeben von Oskar Walzel, Insel Verlag, Leipzig 1910–1915, an Index Volume *(Registerband)* of which appeared in 1920.

INDEX OF GERMAN POEMS

The abbreviations after titles and first lines refer to the principal collections of Heine's poems in which they were published (see chronology): G—Gedichte 1821; L—Buch der Lieder 1827; N—Neue Gedichte 1844; Ro—Romanzero 1851; VS—Vermischte Schriften 1854; Lg—Letzte Gedichte 1869.

(Titles are printed in italic. Chapter titles are in capitals and small capitals.)

INDEX OF TRANSLATIONS

(Titles are printed in italic. Chapter titles are in capitals and small capitals.)